Learning How to Learn

Learning How to Learn

Applied Theory for Adults

Robert M. Smith

Follett Publishing Company
Chicago, Illinois

Atlanta, Georgia • Dallas, Texas
Sacramento, California • Warrensburg, Missouri

Designed by Karen A. Yops

Library of Congress Cataloging in Publication Data

Smith, Robert McCaughan, 1925–
  Learning how to learn.

  Bibliography: p.
  Includes indexes.
  1. Learning. 2. Adult education. I. Title.
LB1060.S64   374   81-17524
ISBN 0-695-81659-4   AACR2

First Printing

Contents

Preface

This book sets forth a concept with far-reaching implications for adults and those who would help adults to change and grow and take advantage of educational opportunities—the learning how to learn concept. Long heralded as desirable, learning how to learn has often proved to be both an intriguing and elusive concept. But now as a result of the experimentation and reflection of many persons in several nations, disciplines, and fields of practice, it appears desirable to offer a comprehensive description of the learning how to learn idea. To be sure, so diverse and complex are the factors to be accounted for that the attempt must be undertaken with considerable humility. The theoretial formulation presented should therefore be regarded as tentative despite the fact that most of the suggested applications derive from research and in-depth experience.

The book's subtitle, *Applied Theory for Adults,* should convey the assumption that a theory of learning how to learn requires direct links to application if it is to prove useful for the dynamic field of social practice called adult education. The organization of the book reflects the interplay between theory and practice. Part I introduces the concept and constitutes the background information for adults seeking to become more successful in learning and for those seeking to help them to do so. Part II treats specific understandings and skills required to take advantage of educational opportunities and how to learn in a variety of settings and ways. In Part III, adult educators who wish to implement the learning how to learn concept with clients will find guidelines, formats, and exercises.

I believe that this effort to draw together learning how to learn research, rhetoric, and experience is warranted because the concept under consideration is of such potential importance to the field that it makes awareness, further research, application, and dissemination essential. For the same contemporary forces that make lifelong learning both a necessity and a reality increasingly impel educators and learners to give higher priority to learning about learning.

The costs in money and energy are dear for individuals who learn inadequately throughout their lives—and most of us do, whatever level of education we may attain. The social costs are surely astronomical and are represented in dropouts, programmatic failure, and inefficient educational delivery systems. One can only guess at the savings that might accrue to an organization that choses to allocate 10 percent of its training resources to helping members learn how to learn, but it seems almost certain that these would be considerable savings indeed.

This book is dedicated to my mentor Paul Bergevin, one of those who has led the way in objectifying the learning how to learn concept.

Among the many colleagues, students, and friends who generously helped with this effort to move toward an applied theory of learning how to learn were the following: David Alexander, Jerry Apps, Carolyn Coulter, Phyllis M. Cunningham, Joan Gorham, Judy Grove, David Gueulette, Kay Haverkamp, Dorothy Jossendal, A. Jean Lesher, Sharan Merriam, John Niemi, Lyn Peterson, Sue Ross, Suzanne Royer, Dennis Sheriff, Patricia Wolf Smith, Sara Steele, Milton Stern, Karen Studniarz, Pat Townsend, Sue Walker, Bud Williams, and Arlene Zoller. Pat Smith's contributions were multifarious.

Robert M. Smith
DeKalb, Illinois

Acknowledgments

Embedded Figures Test figure reproduced by special permission of the publisher, Consulting Psychologists Press, Inc., from the *Group Embedded Figures Test* by Philip Ottman, Evelyn Raskin, and Herman Witkin, © 1971.

Learning cycle from *Theories of Group Process,* edited by C. L. Cooper. London: John Wiley, 1975. Reprinted by permission of John Wiley & Sons, Ltd.

Reprinted with permission of *Convergence,* from "Learning Autonomy: The Second Dimension of Independent Learning" by Michael G. Moore, vol. 5, 1972, p. 82.

Reprinted with permission of the National Association of Secondary School Principals from *Student Learning Styles.* Reston, Va.: NASSP, 1979, p. i.

Figure 3 adapted from Hagberg and Leider, *The Inventurers: Excursions in Life and Career Renewal.* Copyright © 1978. Addison-Wesley, Reading, Mass. Reprinted with permission.

Adapted from *Adult Education Procedures* by Paul Bergevin, Dwight Morris, and Robert M. Smith. Copyright © 1963 by the Seabury Press, Inc. Used by permission of the publisher.

Figure 10 adapted from *Guide to Program Planning* by John McKinley and Robert M. Smith. Greenwich, Conn.: Seabury Press, 1965.

Figure 12 adapted from *Adult Education for the Church* by Paul Bergevin and John McKinley. St. Louis, Mo.: Bethany, 1971.

Appendix B adapted from *Self-Directed Learning* by Malcolm Knowles. New York: Association Press, 1975, pp. 106–07.

Appendix F adapted from *Self-Directed Learning* by Malcolm Knowles. New York: Association Press, 1975.

Appendix G adapted from "Test Anxiety Checklist" by Michael Weissberg. Originally printed in *Cognitive Modification of Test Anxiety: A Leader's Manual.* Counseling and Student Development Center, Northern Illinois University, 1976.

Appendix H adapted from *The Modern Practice of Adult Education* by Malcolm Knowles. Rev. ed. Chicago: Follett Publishing Company, 1980b.

Part I

Theoretical Bases

The underpinnings of the learning how to learn concept are to be found in what we have come to understand about learning, adults as learners, and optimum conditions for the fostering of learning. Critical are the intensely personal nature of the learning process and the demonstrated capacity of adults to assume partial or total responsibility for educating themselves. Research has proven the viability of the notion of learning style. The effects of prior learning and instruction on learning competence in adulthood are becoming increasingly clear; successful ways to improve adults' learning skills are emerging. These matters are central concerns of Part I.

1

A Concept with Important Implications

*I have never ceased learning. . . . After all, what is
education but a process by which a person begins to learn
how to learn?*

Peter Ustinov
Dear Me

*The only man who is educated is the man who has learned
how to learn . . . how to adapt and change.*

Carl Rogers
Freedom to Learn

Both a gifted artist and an internationally known psychologist-educator extol the importance of learning about learning itself. Why?

Because lifelong learning has become a necessity. In an era of breathtaking change, it is truly impossible to acquire early in life the knowledge that adulthood will require. Almost everyone knows this fact.

Because learning itself involves processes, understandings, and skills that can be learned and taught. One *can* learn how to learn more effectively and efficiently at any age.

Because if lifelong learning is absolutely essential and learning how to learn is feasible, then learning about learning takes on real importance. Time and energy given over to it stand to yield rich returns.

Go one step further and you have the rationale for this book. For, just as children never acquire enough education to last throughout adulthood, we adults seldom, if ever, become fully accomplished learners who know how to learn with power in whatever educational situation we encounter. Even the college graduate can be ill-equipped for certain learning tasks and certain educational settings although he or she is obviously better off when compared to the person who lacks such a basic tool for learning as functional literacy.

The adult who has learned how to learn knows the following:

How to take control of his or her own learning.
How to develop a personal learning plan.
How to diagnose strengths and weaknesses as a learner.
How to chart a learning style.
How to overcome personal blocks to learning.
The criteria for sound learning objectives.
The conditions under which adults learn best.
How to learn from life and everyday experience.
How to negotiate the educational bureaucracy.
How to learn from television, radio, and computers.
How to lead and participate in discussion and problem-solving groups.
How to get the most from a conference or workshop.
How to learn from a mentor.
How to use intuition and dreams for learning.
How to help others learn more effectively.

The person who has learned how to learn readily copes with the central task and meaningful activity of life: continuing his or her education. He or she can expect better results from investments in learning and education—more knowledge acquired in less time for less money—and almost certainly will enjoy the learning process more than one who goes about it aimlessly. Moreover, the accomplished learner often has occasion to help others to learn more effectively. Parents can help their children learn how to learn. And teachers and leaders of adults can help their students and clients to learn how to learn.

A Concept with a Pedigree

Learning about learning and helping others to increase their learning power involve two closely related matters: understanding the learning how to learn concept, and putting the implications of that concept to work by applying them to such activities as teaching, training, counseling, program development, and the carrying out of self-directed learning projects.

When we say learning how to learn is a concept, what do we mean?

We mean that it is an important idea. It's no mere everyday conclusion like those that routinely propel our thinking and move us to action (for example, to be firmer with a child, to get more rest, or to cut down on expenditures). It's a notion arrived at by "generalizing from particular instances," as the dictionary puts it. Lifelong learning itself is an example of an educational concept lately come into wide acceptance. Democracy, or the democratic way of life, is a political and social concept with meaning and significance for most of us. ✕

From a concept usually flow certain subconcepts or components. Democracy encompasses such supporting subconcepts as the will of the majority, the rights of minorities, freedom of speech, and the importance of the individual citizen with his or her responsibilities. Democracy and its subconcepts are expressed through specific forms and activities such as representative government, voting, and limiting the length of the terms of officeholders.

The three subconcepts, or components, of the learning how to learn idea are the following: learners' needs (what learners need to know and be able to do for success in learning), learning style (a person's highly individualized preferences and tendencies that influence his or her learning), and training (organized activity, or instruction, to increase people's competence in learning). These supporting ideas of the concept of learning how to learn are interrelated, as we shall see. Like the subconcepts that flow from democracy, they have important consequences—for both educational theory and practice, and implications for program development, teaching, and learning. Much of what follows sets forth the action implications of the learning how to learn concept and its three subconcepts—learners' needs, learning style, and training. (It is essential to note the highly specialized sense in which the term *training* is used throughout this book.)

Learning how to learn comes well recommended. Its validity and utility have probably suggested themselves to innovators for many centuries. We know that Benjamin Franklin found it useful to train the members of the Junto, a discussion club he founded in 1727. Franklin insisted on a set of rules that forestalled dogmatism, minimized conflict, and fostered productive inquiry; rule breakers were assessed fines (Grattan 1959). A distinguished twentieth century writer who also endorsed learning how to learn was Arnold Toynbee, the British historian, who said that learners needed to learn how to transform themselves into "self-teachers" (Tough 1979). John Gardner, a brilliant civil servant and voluntary action leader, calls helping people learn to learn the ultimate goal of the educational system (Gardner 1968). America's best-known educational philosopher, John Dewey, proposed that we evaluate schooling by its success in creating in the student the desire for "continual growth" and in supplying the student with the means for making that desire "effective in fact" (Dewey 1966). A testimonial for the learning how to learn idea by Carl Rogers was presented at the outset of this chapter. Rogers compares one who has learned how to learn to one who has benefited greatly from therapy and to the person who has become truly creative. Edgar Dale devotes an entire chapter to "Learning to Learn" in his provocative book *Building a Learning Environment*. And perhaps the most prestigious book about education to come from UNESCO, *Learning to Be*, stresses the importance of the concept, saying, "learning to learn should not be . . . just another slogan" (Faure 1972, p. 209).

Many distinguished authorities on the education of adults have stressed the importance of learning how to learn. Joseph K. Hart, a leader in the adult education movement in the twenties, talked of teachers being able to "teach their own capacity to learn" (Hart 1926, p. 29). The Canadian adult educator J. R. Kidd writes, "It has often been said that the purpose of adult education . . . is to make of the subject [person] a continuing, inner-directed, self-operating learner" (Kidd 1973, p. 47). Paul Bergevin and several members of the graduate faculty in adult education at Indiana University spent more than a decade developing a widely used approach to collaborative (group) learning that they describe as learning how to learn (Bergevin and McKinley 1971). Cyril Houle devoted his entire book *Continuing Your Education* to coaching adults for successfully continuing their education. Malcolm Knowles takes up the subject in several books, one of which constitutes a resource for helping adults and teachers to alter their assumptions and approaches toward learning (Knowles 1975). Glenn Jensen says, "Teaching adults how to learn is probably a skill that should be an objective of every teacher of adults" (Jensen 1970, p. 519). And Jerold Apps entitles the first chapter of his book *Study Skills: For Those Adults Returning to School,* which is addressed to the returning adult student, "Learning How to Learn."

The mounting concern with learning how to learn can be attributed to the following: (1) a long overdue acceptance of education as a lifelong process that people normally experience, (2) a shift from a preoccupation with teaching to a preoccupation with learning and the study of people learning (mathetics), (3) a proliferation of approaches and techniques for providing adult education—each with its own special requirements, (4) a persistent interest in the notion of learning style, and (5) the research of Allen Tough and many others into adults' self-planned learning.

A concept adjudged so important by prominent leaders within and without the field of adult education clearly has implications for all adults, for their instructors, and for the agencies that provide them with educational opportunities.

Defining the Concept

Because it is an emerging idea, gradually coming into focus, learning how to learn does not mean the same thing to all the writers who underline its importance. For some, the concept centers in mastering those basic skills so vital to most education, such as reading, writing, listening, and study skills. For some, the concept pertains to being more effective at learning and problem solving in groups. For others, it conveys the notion of learners becoming more autonomous or self-directed. For still others, the emphasis is on the individual's processes of perceiving and thinking along with other aspects of learning style. But, as already implied, we have a broader idea in hand, or at least in our grasp. For our purposes here, this definition should do: Learning how to learn involves possessing, or acquiring, the knowledge and skill to learn effectively in whatever learning situation one encounters. If you possess the necessary knowledge and skill, you've learned how to learn; and when you help yourself or others to acquire that kind of knowledge or skill, the concept is also at work.

Some writers prefer the shorter phase *learning to learn*. This phrase is easier to say and to write but loses some of the impact and utilitarian flavor useful in calling attention to the concept and its importance. The chief disadvantage of using the word *how* is that the matters under consideration also include what, why, when, and where to learn; moreover, helping others learn to learn (training) is also part of the concept.

Perhaps some illustrations are in order. The learning how to learn concept becomes operative when—

a person is helped to analyze why he or she is having difficulty with an assignment, or why he or she succeeds with certain learning activities;

a business or industry helps its employees to identify and interpret the various educational opportunities available through the company and in the surrounding community;

a librarian helps a reader to become acquainted with the library's resources and how to gain access to them;

a committee chairperson suggests that the members read and discuss a pamphlet entitled *Better Boards and Committees* before getting on with their main task;

a college provides students with a workshop in study skills;

an instructor asks a student—perhaps after asking, "What did you learn today?" "What did you learn *about learning* today?" or, "How can I be more helpful to you at our next session?";

a person decides to better organize the learning projects he or she carries out at home;

an agency decides *not* to use a method of instruction because its clients lack the learning skills to profit from it;

a church provides training or instruction for the leaders of its study-discussion groups;

an agency takes learning style into account in counseling students about options for instruction;

a professional association provides preconference orientation to members attending their first conference.

To cite a personal example, I recall an experience at age twelve. I had been unable to complete a history project—building a model log cabin—and had gone tearfully to bed at midnight. I awoke to find it finished by my parents who were concerned about my success in school. Although I deeply appreciate that concern, I must admit that their attention to my learning about learning might also have led them to help me understand why I succeeded with some learning tasks but not with others.

We said that three interrelated components—needs, learning style, and training—comprise the learning how to learn concept. We now look at bit more closely at these elements and their relationship.

What the Learner Needs: Requirements for Success

When we describe the person who has learned how to learn as capable of learning efficiently, for many purposes, in a variety of situations, no matter what the method, we confront the question of needs. The concern here is not with basic human needs, like food and affection, but with what people need to know about learning itself for success in learning. Another, slightly narrower, way to put it asks, "What competencies does learning require?" Needs relevant to learning how to learn are of four kinds.

General Understandings. This kind of knowledge helps provide a foundation for the positive attitude and motivation that learning requires. An example that had to be reiterated constantly until very recently is the idea (and fact) that adulthood is prime time for learning. Despite ever increasing levels of participation in adult education activities, many people still have doubts about their ability to learn. They need to understand (and be able to act with conviction on) the fact that learning ability does not decline with age, that frequently it increases.

It is important to know that a wide variety of options for continuing to learn and change lie all about us and within us. We can learn on our own or through an agency for credit, for personal enrichment or for professional development. Many schools and colleges are actively seeking new students by adapting their offerings and services to the problems and interests of adults.

Whether one directs one's own learning or learns through an agency—such as a church, school, college, club, or labor union—it is helpful to know something about adult psychology and the optimum conditions for adult learning. Among other uses, this kind of knowledge is helpful in evaluating the potential usefulness of educational offers tendered by others. It is also important to understand that learning involves processes that can be acquired and enhanced (that learning how to learn pays dividends) and that anxieties and difficulties are to be expected. Finally, most adults are not yet aware that they can take control of learning and increasingly become more self-directed as learners. For, as one writer puts it, "The underlying assumption of learning how to learn is that you, the learner, have the ability and the responsibility for planning much of your own learning" (Apps 1978, p. 1).

Basic Skills. People learn much that is valuable by means other than reading, writing, and arithmetic. But these abilities, along with listening (and, in recent years, viewing), remain central to the learning process. The substantial enterprise called adult literacy, or adult basic education, has come into being to help people who are short of this coin of the learning realm. Of these communication fundamentals, listening and reading stand out as especially significant for success in learning. Operating a computer is also considered by some to be a basic skill for learning and for vocation; "computer illiteracy" has been called a potential national headache (Luehrmann 1980).

Self-Knowledge. It pays to develop awareness and understanding of self as a learner. One can gain valuable insight into personal blocks to learning, to personal strengths and weaknesses, as well as personal preferences for the methods of learning and for learning environments—all key elements in learning style. These factors affect the crucial matter of the attitude one brings to a learning situation. Also important is perspective on the amount of autonomy and structure one prefers and the type of educational setting or mode in which one is most comfortable.

Educational Processes for Three Modes of Learning. Adults usually learn in one of three modes or contexts: self-directed, collaborative, or institutional. The first mode involves carrying out personal learning projects. Collaborative learning is most often found in voluntary organizations, and, as with self-directed learning, credit is seldom a concern. It is sometimes referred to as group learning or as the shared-membership mode. The institutional (or traditional) mode is associated with formalized instruction in such settings as schools and colleges (Blaney 1974).

For success in self-directed learning one needs planning skills for deciding what, when, how, and where to learn; for setting realistic goals; for finding learning resources and choosing and implementing learning strategies. Also central to learning on one's own are overcoming personal blocks to learning, sustaining motivation, estimating progress, and assessing results—all skills that can be acquired or sharpened. Especially important is gaining awareness of the vast array of learning materials and resources, often free, now available in our society.

For success in collaborative learning some of the same kinds of abilities contribute to success. A group that learns or solves problems with ease is one in which the members are adept at planning, conducting, and evaluating their concerted efforts. But the emphasis here is on learning, usually in small, face-to-face groups, to use the experience and expertise of all members to accomplish group tasks and goals. Thus learners' needs include helping skills, sensitivity to the group process, and discussion leadership and participation fundamentals. Groups whose members possess this knowledge and these skills seldom exhibit such dysfunctional symptoms as apathy and destructive group conflict.

In the institutional mode, where credits and degrees become the goals for many and courses and classes the medium, learners have still other kinds of needs. It can be helpful to understand the workings of a college or school itself—of the particular program in which one is enrolled, as well as the support services available to mature students. In institutions that are slow to accommodate to adult students' special interests, problems, and life-styles, adults often have to negotiate the institution, seeking to minimize its constraints and even trying to make it more responsive. Knowing how to study, take notes, write reports and essays, and cope with taking examinations is obviously important. In some institutions, it will be useful to know how to prepare a portfolio to obtain credit for previous experience and nonformal learning.

The broad areas of need that adult learners have concerning learning itself, or requirements for success in learning, are summarized in figure 1. The three areas at the bottom of the figure constitute a foundation for the processes sketched above them.

Learning Style: Everybody Has One

What do we mean by style? It has long been apparent to teachers, educators, and observers that people differ in how they go about certain activities associated with learning. They differ as to how they think. They differ as to how they approach problem solving. They differ as to how they go about "information processing," or putting information through their minds. Some people like to "get the big picture" of a subject first and then build toward a full understanding of that picture by details and examples. Other people like to begin with examples and details and work through to some kind of meaningful construct or way of looking at an area of knowledge out of these details. Some like theory before going into practice. Others don't.

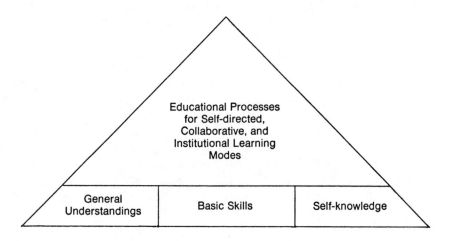

Fig. 1. Needs for Success in Learning

Permit me another personal example. When a group of four other American consultants and I found ourselves quarantined in Nigeria as a result of political and social unrest, we set out to teach ourselves chess. After a time it became clear that I was the only one who had also been reading books on the subject. The others were content to learn by doing. (That their playing was as good as or better than mine naturally made me the victim of good-natured teasing.) Asking myself why I had approached learning a game by way of theory, I realized that this was almost invariably the pattern for me, a key ingredient in my learning style.

Individual differences have always been identifiable and have long interested educators. Much of the recent emphasis on individualizing instruction for both adults and young people stems from this observation. And much of the "streaming," or providing parallel learning sequences, that has gone on in certain kinds of curriculum development has rested on the assumption that people differ in knowledge, experience, attitude, and aptitude. It is also clear that they differ with regard to certain preferences and dispositions, or tendencies, that they have. For example, with regard to method, one might hear a person say, "I don't like discussion," or, "I went to a workshop and we did role playing—it made me uneasy." With field trips, we might hear, "I fall behind and can't hear what the guide is saying." People differ with regard to the amount of structure and autonomy that they want. Some seem to prefer being told what to do at every stage of learning, while some are in the middle, wanting some structure and some freedom of choice. People differ, too, in their reactions to competition. When they find themselves in a seminar where the instructor sets them against each other, some experience great anxiety and even drop out, while others appear to thrive. Environmental considerations also come into play—for example, preferred locations and physical conditions for learning. Some like it hot, some like it cold. The amount of light, background noise, and mobility permitted while learning are relevant factors to consider.

Although individual preferences and dispositions have long been apparent, a growing body of research now emerges that leaves little doubt that there is a sound basis for taking seriously what has come to be called learning style—and that style represents a viable component of the whole learning how to learn concept. People do have identifiable learning styles, and learning styles have important implications for program planning, teaching, and learning.

For those whose style encompasses a preference for definition, *learning style* can be defined as "the individual's characteristic ways of processing information, feeling, and behaving in learning situations."

Training

The third dimension of learning how to learn pertains to deliberate efforts to help people become better at learning and more successful in the educational arena. Despite its frequent use as a synonym for education and the negative associations it carries for some people, the term *training* is extremely useful in understanding the learning how to learn concept and in communicating about the process of helping people to acquire skill in learning and knowledge about education.

The reader who puts the information in this book to work, the instructor who devises memory improvement exercises for students, the consultant conducting a study-skills workshop—all three are involved in training, or have temporarily put on the training hat. Training can be designed to meet the kinds of broad needs and competencies we identified earlier in this chapter. It can pursue a global goal, like understanding the learning how to learn concept itself with its implications for self-directed, collaborative, and institutional learning. It can also deal with such a highly specific matter as how to prepare correspondence study assignments or how to write a learning contract. Training can be built into ongoing instructional situations or stand as a separate event, say as a discussion-skills workshop or a course in speed reading.

Training can last ten minutes or two weeks. Like most any teaching-learning transaction, it can take place in class, at home, or in a retreat or residential situation. But the essence of training, as used here, is that it concerns itself with providing for learning about learning and for improving learning proficiency. It can take place unconsciously, but a degree of purpose and organization needs to be present if we are to distinguish it from random activity, to communicate about it, and to perfect its processes and procedures.

Designing and carrying out training activities can be challenging and rewarding; ingenuity and imagination are often required. The satisfaction of gaining or helping to impart to others knowledge about learning itself can even exceed that usually associated with instruction for other purposes.

Interrelated Subconcepts

Needs, learning style, and training—the three subconcepts of the learning how to learn concept—all are interrelated. We are only beginning to see how, but the outlines are clear. The first, needs, provides a way to focus on specific aspects of learning itself, what might be termed operational aspects as opposed to the more or less automatic processes involved. The focus is on key manageable (and "improvable") processes like planning, evaluating, and communicating. The second, learning style, goes far toward accounting for those individual differences in people that have greatest implication for success in learning. Finally, organized efforts to foster success in learning constitute training. One requires knowledge about the needs and required competencies of the learner in order to train for improved learning performance; knowledge of the individual's learning style is helpful in doing so. A central training task becomes helping learners to gain insight into their styles and make useful adjustments in style.

A three-dimensional model would be necessary to portray the relationship of the subconcepts. Lacking one, we resort to three simplistic diagrams (see figure 2). The first conveys reciprocity; the second, the interpenetrating nature of the relationship; the third, a formula for action that leads to increased competence in learning.

Implications and Applications

There is plenty of evidence that the learning how to learn concept is viable and that translating it into action yields positive results. In a ten-year study and demonstration project, Paul Bergevin and four associates analyzed the strengths and weaknesses of educational programs for adults in churches, libraries, hospitals, and industry. They also initiated and observed some fifty local programs in these same organizational settings to find out how to make them as rewarding and productive as possible for the participants and the organizations. The overriding conclusion reported in the many publications stemming from the Indiana inquiry is the importance of learners' receiving special preparation for the educational tasks they undertake and the approaches they utilize. A major outcome of Bergevin's work has been the development and dissemination of participation training, a system for teaching adults the skills of collaborative learning and group problem-solving (Bergevin and McKinley 1967; McKenzie 1975). Such writers as Leland Bradford and Kenneth Benne have demonstrated convincingly that improved skills for collaborative learning can also result from the T-group experience and other aspects of laboratory learning (Bradford 1964; Benne 1975). In another publication, I described and assessed participation training and laboratory learning as theories of learning how to learn collaboratively (Smith 1976).

Leaders in community development—local self-help study and action programs—report that projects succeed most readily when participants possess discussion, inquiry, and problem-solving skills. A widely publicized community development undertaking is the Antigonish Movement, which had real impact on the lives of farmers and

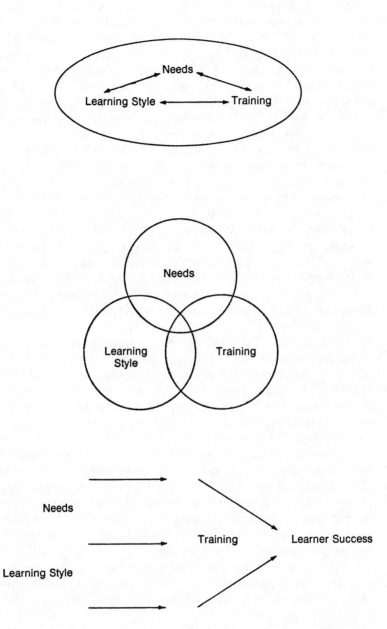

Fig. 2. Interrelations of Subconcepts

fishermen in Nova Scotia as a result of a variety of activities carried on through the extension department of St. Francis Xavier University. In addition to bulletins, radio broadcasts, conferences, and lectures, hundreds of local study-clubs or discussion groups were set in motion. These face-to-face groups have been called the key to the success of the Antigonish program. Not only did relatively unlettered people learn to deal in ideas and consider alternatives, but, when the participants attended rallies and conferences, "men who were never before known to speak in public were able to stand up before large audiences and discuss intelligently the problems of the day" (Laidlaw 1961).

Schools and colleges are taking learning how to learn seriously. After basing curriculum planning on learning style and providing students with a variety of opportunities for improving learning skills, President Joseph Hill of Oakland (Michigan) Community College was able to report dramatic (up to 50 percent) increases in the number of students receiving passing grades in a social science program (Hill 1981). Research at the University of Michigan showed that providing students in correspondence study courses with materials on how to study increased the course completion rate of those enrolled (Wilson 1968). Persons receiving university instruction via telephone were found to learn more effectively after receiving training in appropriate skills (Peterson 1970). Providing a fifteen-week learning strategy course to college undergraduates resulted in up to 31 percent higher posttest scores than those made by control group members ("Practical Applications of Research," *Phi Delta Kappa* vol. 2, no. 2). Community college students in computer science courses got significantly higher grades when they were helped to improve attitudes toward learning and to set personal learning goals (Preising and Frost 1972).

Business and industry make use of the learning how to learn concept by training employees in group problem-solving skills, by counseling them about external educational opportunities, and by endorsing self-directed learning. Malcolm Knowles reports that "top management is buying into self-directed learning fairly generally" for management education and organizational development and "increasingly" for supervisory development (Knowles 1980).

If learning how to learn is essential for learners, what implications stem from the learning how to learn concept for those who provide educational opportunities for adults, who advise them, and who seek to facilitate their learning?

Almost self-evident is the need for the educator of adults to have a working knowledge of the learning how to learn concept—its nature, dimensions, and importance. While he or she may not be able to train individuals in all needed knowledge and skills, the adult educator should be aware of occasions and opportunities for fostering such knowledge and be able to identify situations in which the learning how to learn factor operates. An administrator may not know how people learn most effectively through travel-study and yet insist that a staff member build such learning about learning into the agency's travel-study activities. He or she does not have to possess training knowledge about discussion fundamentals in order to see that such skills training is provided for participants in a discussion group.

Administrators need to understand the programmatic implications of the learning how to learn concept—that learning how to learn activities (training) can be incorporated in the design of courses and workshops, for example. They need to hold before staff members the goal of helping people become more effective learners and ask for evidence of progress toward this goal. They need to take seriously the challenge to devote less time to the development of "content" activities and more time to "process" activities that enable people to become more effective learners. The administrator who acts on the implications of the learning how to learn concept will look at resources and materials, curricula, learning outcomes, teacher performance, and program evaluation in new ways. He or she will seek to ensure that learning how to learn concepts and competencies are stressed in staff-development activities. And adult educators who take learning how to learn seriously will seek to incorporate the concept into agency and program statements about policy and goals.

If an agency conducts orientation for incoming program participants, an ideal opportunity exists to foster learning how to learn. Such orientation may deal with a variety of topics depending on clientele characteristics and program objectives. Adult basic education students will probably require confidence-building exercises, while students in noncredit programs in higher education will probably need to know how to get the most from an instructor. The adult educator needs to realize the importance of devoting time and energy to such activities and of motivating students accordingly.

The educational counselor of adults will have many opportunities to apply the learning how to learn concept. He or she should be aware that lack of learning skills may be responsible for a person's inability to profit from instruction or to get the satisfaction necessary to forestall dropping out. Counselors should be sensitive to counselee behavior that points to learning how to learn deficiencies. They can seek to match learners with learning situations that fit their learning competencies and their learning styles.

The designer of curricula, courses, and other learning experiences can take learning how to learn into account in many ways. As we have seen, if "distance teaching" is utilized (for example, instruction by telephone or correspondence study), provision might need to be made for the acquisition of listening and study skills. Television will not be employed without taking visual literacy into account (Hortin 1980). Those long absent from formal instruction will be offered special assistance when they return to school. And the person recruited to an encounter or other type of personal-growth group will be helped to adjust smoothly to such an intensive experience.

The instructor, the facilitator, and the volunteer aide all have opportunities and responsibilities. They, too, may need to be able to help diagnose the learning problems and learning style of the client. They will want to be aware of the implications of using approaches and methods for which learners have not been prepared: the disadvantage of lecturing to those who are not aural learners; the unfairness of evaluating student reports without describing or modeling a good report; the futility of relying on out-of-class study for persons lacking study skills; the pitfalls of employing the discussion method with people lacking discussion skills.

Having helped adults to diagnose learning problems, the instructor should then become as skilled as possible in helping the learner to overcome or cope with those problems. If learning disabilities are involved, professional help will usually be needed. If skills in discussion or problem solving are needed, the instructor may either attempt to provide them or get outside help. If the learner says, "I have no place to study at home," he or she may be helped by talking about the conditions where he or she lives or about alternative study sites. Instructors can develop their own training skills—skills for helping learners learn more effectively. The instructor will also want to keep before the student the goal of increasing learning skills and provide the kind of feedback that leads toward this goal.

Finally, the learning how to learn concept challenges the expert and the leader in the field of adult education. More research on the concept and its implications is in order (Smith and Haverkamp 1977). We need a clearer picture of learning about learning as a dimension of learning itself. The idea of learning how to learn can be stressed as a condition for optimum adult learning and taught as such in preservice and inservice programs for adult education professionals. We need improved training designs over those described in this book. The training of trainers presents intriguing problems. Policymakers and funding agencies can encourage practitioners to stress learning about learning by offering funding for such efforts and by sponsoring conferences and dissemination efforts.

The major implications and applications of the learning how to learn idea can be summarized this way:

Role	*Implication and Application*
Senior Administrator, Coordinator, Program Developer, Counselor	Stress learning how to learn as a program goal and build a climate of acceptance for it. Provide learning how to learn orientation and training for staff, faculty, and clients. Build the concept into program activities and counseling.
Facilitator, Instructor, Aide, Resource Person, Consultant	Include provision for learning how to learn. Take concept into account in selecting procedures and resources and in evaluation. Give and get feedback about learning-skills development.
University Faculty Member, Other Researcher, State or National Leader, Policymaker	Foster research and dissemination about theory and application of the concept. Incorporate concept into graduate programs for preparing adult education professionals. Help to train trainers who can implement the concept.

Adult educators can also help people become more skilled at learning outside the purview of the educational institution—in carrying out personal learning activities. We know from over thirty recent research studies that for most adults more learning transpires through self-directed efforts than through agency sponsorship. In fact the typical adult spends about 500 hours annually in five independent learning projects. The purposes of these projects vary widely, and the matter learned is almost as diverse as human endeavor itself. The same research that has begun charting this vast subterranean educational territory has identified the kinds of help that agencies can provide the learner interested in improving pertinent learning skills. Allen Tough, the chief spokesman for the research on adults' personal learning projects, has challenged schools and other agencies to adjust programming, goal setting, instruction, and evaluation toward better equipping clients to direct their own learning and conduct learning projects (Tough 1979).

Ronald Gross says that becoming a better lifelong learner is to become more alive, more open to new experiences, ideas, and insights. Because knowledgeable learners understand how to exercise many options and are liberated from educational superstitions (for example, that only institutionalized education is "real" learning), Gross (1977) calls them "free learners."

Of course, important as it is, the learning how to learn idea represents no panacea. Its widespread acceptance and application will never preclude the importance of mystery and wonder, of good luck and good timing (and even of good genes and friends in high places, the less sanguine might observe). But we begin to envision a world of skilled and innovative lifelong learners who possess some of the following characteristics:

Vocation Fulfillment through job and profession for those who seek it; smooth transitions between jobs, roles, and careers; productive workers and managers (but not "robots").

Citizenship People who are informed about the issues, capable of clear thinking, willing to carry their share of the political and social load, and willing to face such awesome responsibilities as the use of power and resources.

Problem solving A society of problem solvers better equipped to cope with personal and family problems and with the problems of organizations, communities, and regions.

Personal growth People who remain open to new experiences and ideas throughout adulthood, who examine life, appreciate the arts, and possess the means for self-expression.

2

The Adult as Learner

Adults enter their schools with very different feelings from children. . . . They attend . . . from their own desire to learn; they understand the value of the work [study] in which they engage; they keep its end in view. . . . Time to the adult learners is precious. . . . In the instruction of adults . . . our conduct . . . should demonstrate to them that we are their sincere friends.

Thomas Pole
A History of the Origin and Progress of Adult Schools

Perceptive people like Dr. Pole have known for centuries that adult learners require understanding and special treatment.

In the previous chapter it was suggested that adults who seek success in learning, and those who would help them, need to understand the characteristics of adult learners and the conditions under which adults learn best. These are the central concerns of this chapter. But first, a word about some key terms we have been using and intend to employ.

In chapter 1, two important concepts were defined: learning how to learn and learning style. Also explained was the special sense in which we are using the terms *needs* (requirements for successful learning) and *training* (deliberate efforts to enhance learning skills and foster success in the educational arena). However, *learning* and *education* were left to fend for themselves.

What Is Learning?

Psychologists and educators don't agree on, or even claim to be able to say with great precision, what human learning is; they are able, however, to describe its effects and how people go about it. A noted authority on adult learning who spent several decades trying to explain learning and synthesize learning theory said that we can only "observe it, note its course and its character, since there is no answer to the question, 'What is learning,' any more than there is to, 'What is electricity' " (Kidd 1973, p. 23). There is, however, general agreement that it has to do with very complex processes—not all the same kind—that involve the mind, the emotions, and the total self, or one's entire being.

Learning has been variously described as a transformation that occurs in the brain; problem solving; an internal process that leads to behavioral change; the construction and exchange of personally relevant and viable meanings; a retained change in disposition or capability that is not simply ascribable to growth; and a process of changing insights, outlooks, expectations, or thought patterns. These are but a few of dozens of attempts at definition, and each highlights or clarifies selected aspects of what is involved in what we call learning.

It has been suggested that the term *learning* defies precise definition because it is put to mulitiple uses. Learning is used to refer to (1) the acquisition and mastery of what is already known about something, (2) the extension and clarification of meanings of one's experience, or (3) an organized, intentional process of testing ideas relevant to problems. In other words, it is used to describe a product, a process, or a function.

When *learning* is used to describe a product, the emphasis is on the outcomes of the experience. After a summer as a camp counselor, for example, a person might be perceived (or perceive himself or herself) as having acquired camping and helping skills, a knowledge of the names of natural objects, an improved understanding of the balance of nature, an appreciation of the value of organized youth activities, and an enhanced sense of self-esteem.

When *learning* is used to describe a process, an attempt is made to account for what happens when a learning experience takes place; it has been called a process of seeking to meet needs and reach goals. Malcolm Knowles's "consensus" definition reads, "[learning is] a process by which behavior is changed, shaped, or controlled" (Knowles 1973).

When *learning* is used to describe a function, the emphasis is on certain important aspects (like motivation), which are believed to help produce learning. The following description stresses function: "Learning is a . . . change that can result when . . . [people] interact with information [materials, activities, experiences]. It occurs to the extent that learners are motivated to change, and it is applied in the real world to the extent they take successful steps to integrate the learning into the real world situation" (McLagan 1978). And also this definition which mentions means to bring change about: "[learning is] based on making connections that relate the new to the familiar" (Botkin 1979, p. 100).

Reflecting on the wide array of available learning theories and definitions of learning, one finds perhaps only one common feature: newness. Something that did not exist or was not grasped has been manifested or brought to light.

It is difficult to be neutral about learning. Differing theories and views of the nature and effects of learning inspire passions and loyalties that have consequences for education and for trying to learn and teach effectively. Priorities are involved. Is it as important to learn math as it is to learn to be able to love and accept others? Isn't the acquiring of an ounce of reverence for life worth a pound of unrelated, meaningless facts? "Simply acquiring information is the lowest level of learning" (Apps 1978, p. 7). And while some writers speak of making everyone a lifelong learner as if it were a holy cause, others say they have a right merely to "be" in the world if that is their choice.

Although learning is clearly complex, involves the mind and emotions, is more or less impossible to define, and gets conceptualized variously, it is nonetheless something we are all familiar with. We have experienced it, we usually "know it when we see it," and we tend to accept its crucial function in life. (Indeed, almost all human behavior can be said to be a result of learning.) Most useful for our purposes here is the highlighting of some generally accepted observations about learning that are clearly relevant to understanding the adult learner and the optimum conditions for adult learning. Here are six.

1. Learning goes on throughout life. To live is to learn. "It's not a task but a way to be in the world" (Robinson 1979). It can be intentional or unintentional. We learn much through the socializing process—from family upbringing, peer influences, work, play, military service, and the mass media. Of course, deliberate efforts to learn are not always made by all persons throughout life, perhaps because such efforts can be difficult, even painful, as well as pleasurable.

2. Learning is a personal and natural process. No one can learn for you. It takes place within you. It is "the process by which we have moved every step of the way since we first breathed"

(Ferguson 1980, p. 288). It seems to be enhanced by the learner's adoption of a "proactive" stance (Knowles 1975) and acceptance of personal responsibility for learning (Bergevin 1967).

3. Learning involves change. Something is added or taken away. "Unlearning" is often involved, especially in adulthood. The change may be as small as attaching a name to a face or as large as making in-depth reorientation in values and self-perception—a "perspective transformation" (Mezirow 1978) or "something of a cultural journey" (Taylor 1980, p. 193). Fear, anxiety, and resistance often accompany and inhibit change.

4. Learning is bound up with human development. Learning affects and is affected by the biological and physical changes in personality, values, roles, and tasks that usually occur over the normal human life span. Learning can give meaning to life's developmental stages with their alternating periods of stability and transition. It is believed that learning helps trigger movement from one stage to the next while constituting a useful way of coping with the sometimes virulent effects of crises and such major changes as retirement or the loss of a spouse.

5. Learning pertains to experience and experiencing. To learn is to experience is to interact with one's environment. Learning is doing. We speak frequently of a learning experience; educators advocate experiential learning. We learn through experience and we can sometimes learn from it. Adults have undergone vastly greater amounts of experience than children, and they normally undergo experience of a different order—having children, engaging in combat, finding and losing jobs, making decisions with far-reaching consequences. The adult's reservoir of past experience represents at one and the same time a potentially rich resource for learning and an obstacle to learning, since learning constitutes in part a process of reaffirming, reorganizing, and reintegrating one's previous experience.

6. Learning has its intuitive side. Knowledge can come from within. Intuition has been called "knowing that can't be tracked . . . without it we would still be in the cave" (Ferguson 1980, p. 296). Some of our most important and creative insights can come through tacit knowing, through the subconscious, by letting problems and ideas simmer, by paying attention to the seemingly unrelated, and through meditation. Some people even

develop strategies for using dreams to help in personal decision-making. Recent research concerning the functioning of the brain is providing a physiological basis and impetus for taking seriously this aspect of learning.

Learning, then, is an activity of one who learns. It may be intentional or random; it may involve acquiring information or skills, new attitudes, understandings, or values. It usually is accompanied by changes in behavior and goes on throughout life. It is often thought of as both processes and outcomes. *Education* can be defined as "the organized, systematic effort to foster learning, to establish the conditions, and to provide the activities through which learning can occur."

What Is Adult Education?

While it doesn't present quite the problems that attend the definition of learning, the term *adult education*—with its multiple meanings and synonyms—presents its own difficulties. The term is used in at least three ways.

The first way it is used is to describe a process through which people continue to learn after formal schooling ceases. Examples might be reading, traveling, and viewing films. This usage clearly allows *education* and *learning* to overlap. The second is to refer to the organized activities that agencies and institutions provide for adults. And the third is to convey the idea of a field of social practice or a movement. Thus we may hear it said that adult education has come into its own in recent years (Knowles 1977, p. viii).

The rapid spread of courses of study to prepare people for careers as educators of adults gives rise to yet another use of the term as a field of study; thus one can major in adult education just as in elementary education, history, social work, or library science.

The overall concept or umbrella term *adult education* is not always used. Some people prefer *continuing education* or, more recently, *lifelong learning*. The former is more likely to refer to the educational activity of professionals—nurses, teachers, or lawyers, for example. Although neither term carries the negative connotation that adult education has for some people because of its long association with literacy and remediation, neither is likely to replace the latter as the umbrella term. Most of the other terms one encounters are associated with specific institutions and providers of education for adults and seem likely to remain so, for example, terms such as *postsecondary education, extension,* and *nontraditional education* (colleges and universities); *training and development* (business, industry, and government); and *community education* (public schools).

As for the concept of adulthood (and Who is an adult?), the person who regards himself or herself as an adult and has assumed the responsibilities associated with adulthood (worker, spouse, parent) is considered to be an adult and, therefore, is fair game for adult educators and likely to learn best under conditions that take into account the characteristics of adults as learners.

For our purposes, then, *adult education* refers to a purposeful effort to foster learning by persons who have become largely responsible for their own comings and goings, in other words, adults. *Adult educators* are persons who seek to help adults learn and provide them with educational opportunities.

Four Critical Characteristics of Adult Learners

The literature of adult education contains a great deal of information about the nature of adult learners, how they differ from children and youth as learners, and the implications for practice. But for learning how to learn—becoming a more effective learner and helping others to do so—a minimum requirement is a working grasp of the four essential characteristics of adult learners explored next.

A Different Orientation to Education and Learning.   Children, to oversimplify, spend their time either at play or at school. Adults have multiple roles, tasks, responsibilities, and opportunities. Unless required to do so by an employer, a judge, a relicensing authority, or a draft board, adults may participate in education or they may do something else like work, entertain, golf, shop, or watch television. When they do participate, as Thomas Pole observed almost two hundred years ago in British literacy classes, they usually bring a special orientation to learning that arises out of a different orientation toward living. That they bring different feelings and "attend from their own desire," Pole found significant, as have many writers ever since.

In addition to their options and the demands on their time, there is the matter of how adults perceive time and their time of life. "Time to the adult is precious," said Pole. During one's thirties and forties, one's time to live becomes increasingly seen as finite, with implications for how to spend it, and for considering such matters as changing careers or returning to school. Kidd expresses it this way:

> Adults have more stable interests and a different perception
> of time. They are able to internalize long-range goals and
> work toward them over a period of time. On the other hand,
> many adults as well as youth live in the here-and-now and

will seldom work toward distant goals unless they themselves have a commitment to these goals. To the old what time is left may appear very short, and to be valued, perhaps even to be hoarded, rather than spent. Howard McClusky has pointed out that the adult's view of himself—his self-adequacy—is very closely linked with his view of time. "I am too old," "If I were twenty years younger," may be ways in which the adult is not only talking about his chronological age but also stating what he feels about his own capacity.

For an adult, more than for a child, the investment of time in an activity may be as important a decision as the investment of money or effort. (Kidd 1973, p. 48)

That "view of self" referred to by Kidd becomes of real significance with regard both to participating in education and to profiting from it. Adults tend to see life from the perspective of an "ever-increasing past; a fleeting, pressured present, and a finite future." The perception of a "fleeting, pressured present" may drive them toward education or away. It exerts pressure for resolving conflicts and solving problems, but it also "involves conflicting concerns, needs and desires which can become essential content in the learning process." The adult has a "firmer and more fully formed" self-concept than does the child. Self-concept is how one might describe oneself; self-esteem is how one feels toward self (Brundage and MacKeracher 1980). This permits holding up a potential educational experience, a learning objective, or an idea against the idealized self that one might wish to become or try to maintain.

Perhaps the most essential component of the self in relation to learning is self-seen-as-learner. If the adult thinks that learning and the adventure of change are as much a part of his life as his work and family roles, he will be more likely to enter into learning and achieve a higher level of intellectual performance. If the adult thinks that learning is only for children or is a nonresponsible status in society, he will likely not participate willingly in learning activities. The self-seen-as-learner role also appears to be an essential component in learning how to learn. (Brundage and MacKeracher 1980, p. 35)

It is often said that because of time pressures, multiple options, and adults' own views of themselves, they are most likely to engage in education and to profit most from learning activities that are practical and problem centered. There is considerable truth to this notion. How-

ever, efforts to promote courses on social issues and community problem-solving have usually met with frustration. And as people search
for novelty and for meaning in life, they often turn to education for
help in discovering and releasing their unused potentials and capacities as well as for patently practical reasons.

One unequivocal implication of adults' different orientations toward
life and of their broader experience bases is that they can usually
identify or help to identify what they need to learn.

An Accumulation of Experience.   Adults obviously enjoy the potential benefits and drawbacks of more accumulated life experience
than children. Much of this experience is qualitatively different from
that of children. It derives from a wide range of roles and responsibilities. A single individual at a single point in life can be a worker,
supervisor, lay preacher, trustee, scout leader, and part-time student.
He or she can be simultaneously a son or daughter, parent, and grand-
parent.

The accumulated experience usually includes many events of impact
and stress. Adults are apt to have the foundations of their lives
stripped away from time to time.

> The college dorm is not the same as the room back home.
> Leisurely afternoons are burned away by the new born baby.
> Jobs are lost. Parents die. Ideals are tarnished. Divorces oc-
> cur. Bodies don't perform as they once did. Children leave
> home. The stock market crashes. Responsibilities are taken
> away. Retirement becomes mandatory. Mates die and leave
> them alone. (Davis and McCallon 1975, p. 26)

Despite many similarities in adult roles and responsibilities, the sum
of each person's experiences makes for uniqueness. No two persons
have had quite the same experiences in exactly the same way. Specialized talents and interests develop. Ways of supporting present values
and beliefs and in reacting to new information become increasingly
differentiated. A representative sample of adults in their fifties is more
varied in learning ability than a representative sample of those in their
twenties (Knox 1977). The members of a group of adults may appear
to be quite similar, but actually they are much more heterogeneous
than a group of children. A class or discussion group made up of
adults, even with similar job titles (nurses) or life roles (mothers), is
likely to contain great variety in energy, extent of knowledge about
what is to be learned, and motives for accepting or rejecting new ideas
or procedures. This uniqueness affects one's preferences for modes of
learning and learning environments and thus helps form the basis for
the learning style concept.

Eduard Lindeman, adult education's venerated spokesman, saw the chief purpose of learning as discovering the meaning of our experience, calling this effort a "lifelong quest of the mind." In this view one learns in order to make sense out of the vast experience inevitably accumulated through living—certainly a major purpose for learning.

If it seems clear that past experience will affect our orientation toward and response to education, either for avoiding it or coming to it with positive or negative feelings, we are still confronted with trying to understand the role of the adult's broad formulation of experience in the learning process itself. The significant role of past experience shines through in psychologist David Ausubel's (1968) contention that what the learner already knows is the most important factor influencing learning. But how does experience make its presence felt? When is it helpful and when does it hinder? Something like the following seems to happen in the learning situation itself. Donald Brundage and Dorothy MacKeracher summarize what is an admittedly complex and obscure process.

> Past experience . . . determines what information will be selected for further attention and how it will be interpreted; and determines what meanings, values, strategies and skills will be employed first. If these are found to be suitable, new learning will proceed efficiently and productively. If these are found to be unsuitable, the adult will first search back through all previous experience for some suitable material which can be applied indirectly. If nothing can be found, the adult is faced with a considerable challenge: to acknowledge the inadequacy of [presently possessed] meanings, values, skills, and strategies. (Brundage and MacKeracher 1980, pp. 32–33)

In this last case, the learner's self-concept as a competent person may well be threatened. He or she can turn off temporarily or even withdraw altogether ("rejecting the validity, value and necessity of learning anything") rather than risk going ahead for "an unknown transformation of that self concept." Brundage (p. 33) goes on to say that the adult's fund of past experience brings about a learning process that "focuses on modifying, transferring, and re-integrating meanings, values, strategies, and skills, rather than forming and accumulating as in childhood."

Past experience then constitutes a base for new learning and a source of obstacles discouraging deliberate entrance into education or hampering learning and change once in. It often requires "unlearning" and helping adults to raise their established meanings, values, skills, and strengths to a conscious level, and to examine these meanings, values, skills, and strengths and proceed to a new awareness, to the perception of new relationships and new insight about themselves as learners. And, as many of history's exceptional teachers have demonstrated, experience enables adults to learn through analogy and figures of speech.

A final effect of the adult's accumulation of experience is to make adult learners themselves very important resources for learning. They can often direct their own learning and learn a great deal from each other.

Special Developmental Trends. The term *development* refers to more or less orderly, predictable, and sequential changes in characteristics and attitudes. Studies of adult development have revealed that adults pass through developmental phases that are different from those experienced by children and youth. Involved are continuous individual growth and change together with periodic change in orientations, assumptions, and patterns of relationship. Adult development theories focus on age-related matters in physical (e.g., energy level), psychological (e.g., cognition), and social (e.g., family) areas; specific events in a time frame (e.g., entering the world of work); or the development of a personality trait (e.g., moral maturity). Most theories distinguish between periods of stability (involving consolidation and preparation for future change) and periods of transition (destabilization and movement to another phase).

Developmental theory often divides adulthood into various periods or stages. One of the most common and manageable divisions is early adulthood (18–39), middle adulthood (40–59), and later adulthood (over 60). These periods can then be differentiated in terms of most commonly encountered activities, preoccupations, problems, and interests. In *Passages,* Gail Sheehy identifies six stages and provocatively calls them Pulling Up Roots, The Trying Twenties, Catch 30, Rooting and Extending, The Deadline Decade (the Forties), and Renewal or Resignation.

The developmental tasks typically confronting people at each stage have been identified. Havighurst (1972) defines such a task as one which "arises at or about a certain period in the life of an individual, successful achievement of which leads to . . . happiness and success with later tasks." Failure to negotiate a task can result in unhappiness, social disapproval, and difficulty with later tasks. Tasks derive from and are associated with systems and roles. Roles stem from membership in age and gender groups, family, occupations, and religious and other social groups.

In his summary of the research on adult development and its relation to adult learning, Alan Knox focuses on "change events" (called "marker events" and "life events" by others) such as leaving home and retirement. These significant happenings periodically punctuate the relative stability of adult life and can significantly alter our relationships, our self-concepts, our use of time, and our morale. The events, which can represent either losses or gains, may entail either increased vulnerability or increased potential for positive change. People can react by feeling overwhelmed, withdrawing, seeking assistance, or even by forming and activating plans for using their potential. However, while major change events can produce such positive effects as increased motivation for community service and for education, several such events happening together may result in a trauma like the notorious midlife crisis (Knox 1977).

During periods of transition or following major change events, adults appear receptive to education and learning related to reassessing personal goals, reasserting themselves as valued members of society, and reconfirming their self-esteems. The more significant and potent transitions require learning that allows adults to explore their personal meanings and values and to transform those meanings and values in ways that make them more congruent with reality. This is sometimes called qualitative learning. Relatively stable periods and stages are times for broadening and consolidating knowledge and for integrating new meanings into old constructs and life experience.

A national sample of 2,000 persons over twenty-five found 83 percent of them learning in order to cope with a life change. Fifty percent of the transitions requiring learning were career related, 16 percent were family related, and 13 percent were related to new leisure patterns (Aslanian and Brickell 1980). Transitions trigger learning in three major ways.

1. A change in our life circumstances may occur unexpectedly, requiring us to learn rapidly in order to adapt to the situation.

2. Slower transitions may allow us more comfortable accommodation to change by stimulating us to learn as the transition occurs.

3. After a period of life review we may choose to make changes and prepare for these through anticipatory learning. (McCoy 1980, p. 76)

Successful negotiation of transitional periods can be facilitated by awareness that transitions are normal. People need suggestions for alternate ways of making transitions. Returning to school appears to be not so much a transition in itself as a consequence of another change (actual or anticipated) in one's circumstances (Aslanian and Brickell 1980). And the realization that one stands at an appropriate point for major reassessment and direction finding can move a person to participate in life-planning activities that can take the form of group learning, counseling, or working through exercises on one's own.

Counseling can be especially useful during transitions and following major change events. It can help prevent panic and assuage loneliness, ventilate feelings, clarify problems, and explore coping mechanisms, problem solutions, and opportunities for change and growth. Counseling may be in order before, during, or after other organized learning activity is resorted to (Knox 1977).

Anxiety and Ambivalence.   Ideally we would all possess such security and self-understanding that change and even major reorganization of the self could be undertaken without anxiety. But adults typically confront educational opportunity and participate in learning with mixed feelings and even with fear. Understanding these reactions can help one to learn more effectively and assist others to do so.

We live in an ambiguous and paradoxical world, a world that is filled with diversities, contradictions, and dilemmas. We are both other-centered and ego-centered. We want to serve and to be useful, while at the same time getting, at the very least, our share. We want to win while being a good sport. We want to obey and to bend the law. We want the security of family and the freedom of singleness. We want the glamour of youth and respect for our age. And we simultaneously cling to tradition and reach out to seek the new, to change while remaining stable.

One area of paradox and ambivalence with special relevance for how we approach education and learning concerns autonomy. Kidd (1973) calls dependence "the badge of the student." A large portion of the literature of education deals with such matters as freedom, control, authority, and autonomy as they relate to the roles of teacher and student. Adults apparently have deep-seated needs to move toward autonomy and self-direction and to be so perceived by self and others. Normal adult development involves a gradual increase in personal willingness to take responsibility for guiding one's life based on values and ideas chosen by oneself (Fales and Greey 1980–81).

While we strive for independence, we also retain throughout life our dependency needs. We require the approval and support of others in order to preserve our sense of well-being. We accept leadership in areas where we lack experience or expertise. We need to ask for help when we've lost the way. Independence and autonomy are good. They help reduce our sense of powerlessness and improve our self-confidence and self-esteem. But dependence also has its uses; and so does interdependence—the sharing of effort, responsibility, and rewards in the manner of athletes in team sports. When adult learners have too little autonomy, their dignity can be affronted, their motivation inhibited, and their pleasure in learning stifled. But learners suddenly confronted with more responsibility for their own learning than they expected or are used to usually respond with anxiety, and sometimes withdrawal.

As we shall see in later chapters, training for learning effectiveness can involve assisting adult learners to become more self-directed if they are to conduct personal learning projects, to become constructively interdependent if they will be learning collaboratively, and to cope with the shifting autonomy-dependency requirements of schools and colleges.

Another paradox arises from our tendencies to maintain stability and also to change in directions we deem desirable. Considerable change automatically comes into our lives by way of living—through a changing environment, biologically determined processes, and the stages, transitions and change events of the life cycle. Life's changes produce stress, and too much in too short a time can produce harmful stress. Education calls people forth to change. With their experience and insight, however, adults can usually envision the potential for dislocation and stress inherent in such a major decision as returning to full-time student status or undertaking a career change.

Learning itself is not passive absorption but an active process of transmuting new knowledge, values, and skills into behavior. There is usually some discomfort, even pain, involved in giving up that with which we have become comfortable. Learning can demand a "temporary surrender of security" (Sheehy 1976). Even after having made a voluntary decision to engage in learning, we resist remaking ourselves. We often seek to defend present behavior by mechanisms such as strongly reasserting it, finding reasons to justify it, or even by anger or withdrawal.

Thus the ambivalence we feel toward commitments to education and toward the content and processes of teaching and learning activities. In group learning situations this ambivalence can be faced and constructively resolved through the possession of a positive self-image and a climate in which others don't insist that individuals change, learners are allowed to express themselves freely, and learners feel genuinely accepted and are not put on the defensive (McKinley 1978).

Despite all the evidence to the contrary, many adults still harbor doubts about their personal learning ability. Capacities tend to be underestimated and underused (Knox 1977). Family members, friends, or acquaintances may reinforce the adult learner's self-doubts by questioning his or her abilities, motives, or need for a certain kind of knowledge. Later adulthood and old age are periods when people are especially prone to this source of anxiety. For adults to undertake a return to school or an in-depth learning project is to move into unknown territory regardless of their educational level and personal resources.

Early schooling has been charged with fostering anxiety toward learning. According to Donald Rogers, "The subject we may be teaching most in our schools is fear." Rogers lays the blame on overemphasis on achievement and the communicating of adult anxieties to children (Roberts 1975, p. 27). In one workshop, every adult asked to recall an important school incident chose a negative or traumatic event (Ferguson 1980, p. 283).

Carlos Castaneda's wise man, Don Juan, describes anguish that can accompany learning.

> A man goes to knowledge . . . as he goes to war, wide awake, with fear. . . . He slowly begins to learn—bit by bit at first, then in big chunks. His thoughts soon clash. What he learns is never what he pictured, or imagined, and so he begins to be afraid. . . . Every step of learning is a new task, and the fear begins to mount. . . . Fear! A terrible enemy—treacherous and difficult to overcome. (Castaneda 1968, p. 326).

During a period of crisis (e.g., following loss of job), when the ego is already under stress, fear, and anxiety may be highest. A major effect of anxiety is distraction from the learning tasks because our faculties are put to work mobilizing personal defenses (McKinley 1978). Also, if stress is too high, adults may find it difficult to communicate effectively in learning situations. Some adults display high "oral communication apprehension" and try to avoid oral communication (McCrosky and Anderson 1976).

Adults may also react with apprehension to a specific area of content. Many are prone to math anxiety. The special anxieties attending learning of a second language have been well documented. Some of this anxiety and its attendant resistance to learning is believed to result from adults' negative reactions to the need for almost complete dependence on others (e.g., a teacher) in the early phases of language learning (Curran 1976).

Methodology poses problems too. People may be uncomfortable with certain techniques (e.g., role play), certain tasks (pronouncing foreign words aloud), certain environments (a nurse in the presence of a physician), or pieces of equipment (a videotape player). Adults tend to undergo much more stress than youth in testing situations; many even postpone application to advanced study to avoid taking the Graduate Record Examination. They can fear both revelation of ignorance and negative comparisons with peers. They may even feel guilty about their own expectations or excessively high standards for themselves (Kidd 1973).

Learners, then, need to seek and educators need to help provide a learning climate that minimizes anxiety and fosters confidence. While some tension is normal, even desirable for stimulating challenge and bringing out capacities, educators should avoid or seek to modify approaches and requirements likely to have negative effects. The rusty learner will need training to revive capacities and overcome excessive anxiety, and someone encountering a method for the first time or an unfamiliar subject will often need special preparation.

Six Optimum Conditions for Learning

Adults are characterized by a special orientation to life, living, education, and learning; a relatively rich experience base to draw on and cope with; different developmental changes and tasks than preadults; and their own brand of anxiety and ambivalence. These essential characteristics generate some optimum conditions for adult learning—conditions that educators find useful to activate and that learners have a right to expect. The conditions cited next are especially relevant to learning how to learn and helping others to do so. Adults learn best when these six conditions are met.

1. *They feel the need to learn and have input into what, why, and how they will learn.* Voluntary participation is almost always preferable to mandatory participation; however, people do sometimes perceive learning as necessary after being forced into it. When they are adequately prepared or trained, their input takes the form of directing or sharing in processes for needs analysis, goal setting, resource and strategy selection, and evaluation. "Involve the learner" has long been a watchword of adult educators. Adequate preparation (training) for involvement has not always been provided.

2. *Learning's content and processes bear a perceived and meaningful relationship to past experience and experience is effectively utilized as a resource for learning.* Adult learners need to realize that their experience constitutes both a potential asset and a potential liability for learning. Adult educators need to take learners' previous experiences into account in selecting methods and materials, in making presentations, and in helping

learners to modify and transform the meanings and skills derived from their previous experiences. Persons providing training can relate the need for learning about learning to people's past experiences and create environments in which people are free to analyze experience and try out new ways of learning.

3. *What is to be learned relates optimally to the individual's developmental changes and life tasks.* Educators can use knowledge of developmental processes and chronologically oriented stages in programming, instruction, and counseling if they bear in mind that individuals vary widely in the extent to which they conform to developmental trends. Individuals wishing to become more effective learners can gain useful personal perspectives on themselves as learners and potential learners through exposure to developmental knowledge and theory.

Learning about philosophy, and how to perform the activities of philosophers, obviously requires possession of more complex concepts and processes than learning how to sweep. A person may be lacking in higher levels of cognitive development (e.g., the ability to apply concepts and principles) either as a result of never having attained them or of repression due to environmental pressures to function at a lower level. Appropriate training and instructional design can help learners compensate if deficiencies are not too great for the learning purposes and tasks at hand.

4. *The amount of autonomy exercised by the learner is congruent with that required by the mode or method utilized.* As mentioned in chapter 1, the mode can be self-directed, collaborative, or institutional with the first requiring the most autonomy and the last the least. Within a mode, an activity such as writing a research paper obviously requires more autonomy than working on class exercises in the presence of an instructor. Training helps learners to deal with the problems attending autonomy-related aspects of a particular mode, method, or activity (e.g., making learners more independent for self-directed learning and interdependent for collaborative learning).

5. *They learn in a climate that minimizes anxiety and encourages freedom to experiment.* Ben Franklin took climate into account when he declined to have the Junto's meetings in a tavern but consented to the members' downing a glass of wine before

moving from one discussion topic to another. Those who direct their own learning bear most of the responsibility for establishing climate and usually must consider matters such as the physical environment of the home and the possible effects of asking certain others to help them. Collaborative learning requires a climate of mutual trust and teamwork in which people feel accepted and free to disagree and take risks. In traditional settings, instructors set climate by their attitudes, assignments, and reaction to individuals' efforts to learn. It has been said that a successful climate for learning is almost assured when people are truly treated as adults.

6. *Their learning styles are taken into account.* As we shall see in chapter 3, this may be done formally through the use of diagnostic instruments, or informally by paying attention to people's preferred ways of processing information and preferred learning environments.

Four Special Populations

It will be asked if our four generalizations about the salient character-istics of adult learners and six optimum conditions for learning apply evenly to adults of all ages and backgrounds—to the undereducated as well as the Ph.D., to the twenty-year-old and the eighty-year-old alike. A brief examination of four special populations, all major clientele groups for adult educators, should yield an answer.

The Undereducated. It has been said that students in literacy pro-grams are, in their essential characteristics, like everyone else (Manzo et al. 1975). However, while there are healthy, well-adjusted, even wealthy illiterates, adults deficient in basic skills may be prone to economic and health problems, learning disabilities, low self-esteem, and a sense of powerlessness. They may lack faith in education as a prime source of potential help with personal and community problems. Once enrolled in educational programs, they are four times more likely to drop out than other groups. They do, however, carry out almost as many self-directed learning projects as middle-class people (Tough 1980). Efforts to involve them in other kinds of learning may require them to reorder their perceptions of their world and their potential role in it (Freire 1974). Bringing about their successful involvement in planning and evaluative processes will probably be more difficult than with middle-class people and others with greater amounts of formal education. Feringer (1979) finds "indigent" students largely incapable of educational planning, but some teacher training materials show how it can be done ("What Is the Teacher Student Role in ABE?" 1975).

These adults are less likely to respond to programming related to developmental tasks, but strong family feelings often provide a basis for motivation (e.g., learning in order to help their children learn). The nature of much of their experience may be unfamiliar to those helping them to learn, and their previous experiences will inhibit their meaningful processing of information presented by those who fail to take this into account. Despite the fact that they have already demonstrated skill in learning in order to have survived, these adults are especially subject to anxiety and doubts about learning ability when entering formal education situations.

> Placing his foot on that first step of the schoolhouse is a giant stride for the adult illiterate. To go into the room and sit at a desk demands as much courage for the illiterate as is required of a soldier in the heat of battle. . . . [They have to be helped to overcome] their worst fears about themselves—that they *could not learn.* (Bowren and Zintz 1977, p. 21)

The establishment of a climate for minimizing anxiety thus becomes the most crucial condition for learning success in this population.

Those Returning to College.   Compared with the undereducated or disadvantaged, these persons, the majority female, tend as a group to have fewer problems with health and resources and to be somewhat less prone to feelings of helplessness and doubts about the efficacy of education. Some have had recent success in a delayed completion of high school. They usually recognize a need to learn, but unless the higher education institution has made efforts to take their world and life-style into account, they are committing themselves to an environment likely to produce considerable anxiety. After years of other preoccupations requiring different skills, they must adapt to the requirements and tasks of a competitive arena that prizes objectivity, critical thinking, and accurate expression (usually written expression in "academic prose"), one which often uses rigorous examinations. Many of their fellow learners are recent high school graduates and better prepared for some of the tasks at hand.

Returning students are not so much prone to doubts about learning ability as to misgivings that they can keep up, meet all the requirements, and follow through to a degree or other personal goal. And they will usually be subject to heavy outside pressures arising from employment, parenthood, community work, housework, or the reaction of spouses to their decision to return. A major life change, transition, or developmental task is probably involved in that decision. The decision, especially in the case of returning women, often leads to a major "reordering of reality" and a redefinition of personal values and personal potentialities (Mezirow 1978).

Even when higher education institutions do provide nontraditional programs and adult degrees, other problems arise—problems related to self-doubt and autonomy and to expectations about education and learning.

Returning students are not new, just more numerous than ever before. Vera Brittain describes her return to Oxford after a four-year interruption to serve as a volunteer army nurse in World War I. She believed, erroneously, that her instructors would "concede to her the privileges of maturity" and feel an interest in someone with "first hand experience of the greatest event of their generation" (Brittain 1980).

The experience of most persons returning to college is likely to be more congruent with that of those helping them learn than is the case with the undereducated and their instructors, affording the former more opportunity to utilize experience in processing information and relating new meanings to old. Adult undergraduates show stronger capabilities than eighteen-, nineteen-, and twenty-year-olds for conducting analytical inquiry, for integrating and synthesizing theoretical materials, and for independent study activities (Kasworm 1980). Involving these adult undergraduates in planning and evaluative processes should not present major problems. They can serve as resources for each other and come (with guidance) to look on faculty as resource persons rather than overwhelming authority figures. They can learn to manage time effectively, become more assertive about their rights, and negotiate the institution's bureaucratic hurdles.

The Professional. These persons have relatively high incomes, access to resources, and a variety of life-styles. They are the most likely as a group to continue their education (Aslanian and Brickell 1980, p. 46). They are better established in their communities, more mobile, and more confident of their abilities (including the ability to learn) than a cross section of the general population. However, they feel heavily pressed for time, and their careers tend to absorb a great deal of their time and energy. Since they are often disenchanted with formal education, they could be expected to be motivated to direct their own education. However, their preprofessional education may have left them ill-equipped to do so as a result of its emphasis on authoritative presentation of information and encouragement of dependency relationships with teachers.

Professionals' work almost automatically demands some intentional learning; they report that 70 percent of their most useful job-related learning occurs through personal and collegial problem-solving activity. Their decision to participate in continuing professional education is usually made on a basis of personal attitudes toward this kind of learning and the expectations of superiors and others. A good deal of it is mandated or quasi-mandated despite the absence of research demonstrating positive payoff from such activity.

About 50 percent of professionals surveyed report engaging in non-career-related education pertaining to such matters as hobbies and recreation, foreign languages, current affairs, and psychology. Professionals exhibit a wide range of motives for participation in general or leisure education, but they are especially interested in getting a change from the job environment. They are less interested than other groups in new careers, certification, and becoming better family members. The major self-perceived barriers of learning of professionals in order of importance are not enough time, job responsibilities, and, surprisingly perhaps, cost. Doubt about learning ability ranks near the bottom (Houle 1980).

While few professionals doubt their own learning ability, their participation and learning are affected by the need to avoid revealing professional incompetence in public. For this reason some providers of continuing education for physicians mail the individual a quiz over a topic in which he or she has shown interest. The doctor returns the answer sheet, which is held in confidence, and then receives material to study that pertains to revealed gaps in knowledge.

With regard to the role of experience in learning, the professional possesses a technical vocabulary and specialized frames of reference for relating new information to old. That same experience base can become a handicap in learning for other than job-related purposes such as achieving self-understanding or improving interpersonal relationships. The professional can be expected to have adequate levels of cognitive development for most learning endeavors.

When it comes to involving professionals in planning and evaluative processes, obstacles arise. These learners are usually capable of meaningful involvement. However, they may feel that time pressures and the need for precise, problem-centered information make it necessary for authorities to diagnose needs, set the objectives, and determine the learning activities for continuing education programs. Those in the helping professions that stress interpersonal relationships—clergy, social workers, and counselors, for example—are most likely to respond positively to efforts to actively involve them in these processes.

Professionals, then, tend to be in possession of the tools for learning, to do considerable learning on their own, and to be wary of opportunities for input into processes, especially where job-related learning is concerned. Collaborative learning is not as appealing (and perhaps appropriate) for them as the traditional and self-directed modes. A lead-ing authority on continuing professional education has recently stressed the importance of self-directed learning by this population (Houle 1980).

The Older Person.   People over sixty tend to be especially concerned with income, health, adjustment to retirement of themselves or their spouses, and with retaining a sense of usefulness and purpose. With the undereducated they share tendencies toward feelings of decreasing control, even helplessness, especially when faced with institutional care. Many highly stressful events occur at this time of life—loss of a spouse, forced retirement, and a sharp reduction in income to name a few. Participation rates in organized educational programs decline sharply. Level of education and socioeconomic status affect the extent to which these persons are interested in education for self-expression, as opposed to education for coping.

Developmental changes obviously tend toward declines in energy and difficulties in seeing and hearing. The potential of past experience for both positive and negative effects on learning peaks in old age. This phenomenon has its causes in the mass and diversity of the experience base and the more rigid values, attitudes, and frames of reference through which new information is processed. Opportunity to apply previous experience directly is especially important in older adults (Brundage and MacKeracher 1980). Older persons often find it more difficult to focus on the specifics of current experience and on future expectations than on past experience itself. Those who did not avail themselves of growth opportunities during the middle years may ex-hibit "intellectual aging" and generalized loss of confidence in learning ability. Fortunately research and experience are showing that intellec-tual aging is reversible and not necessarily a barrier to learning. The time perspective of older adults and their larger experience base are frequently cited as reasons for focusing instruction on the eliciting of understanding of what is already present within them.

Although it might appear relatively difficult to do so with older adults, educational gerontologists are calling for their active involve-ment in planning and evaluative processes. Laboratory training and other consciousness-raising techniques are also being prescribed for them by experts as alternatives to innocuous learning activities that have little impact on self-concept, self-understanding, and coming to terms with death. And studies of self-directed learning or personal learning projects show that older adults are not far behind those adults in their middle years in the number undertaken (Sherron and Lumsden 1978).

Learning conditions of greatest relevance for this population would appear to be those dealing with the establishing of a climate of security and trust, the relating of past experience meaningfully to new experience, and encouraging perception of the need to learn.

Descriptions of special adult populations could be extended to such other groups as the handicapped, the young adult, and English-as-a-second-language students. But this brief application should make it clear that adult learners do share common characteristics to which our six optimum learning conditions apply, unevenly but consistently. For effective, meaningful learning to occur, their application will need to be made with sensitivity, judgment, and ingenuity.

Effects of Learning and Instruction
on Learning How to Learn

> The content for every learner in every educational activity influences the learner's skills in, or attitude toward, learning. (Bergevin, McKinley, and Smith 1964, p. 273)

In addition to specific training for learning-skills improvement, what contributes to adults' acquiring the desire to learn and skill in learning, what kind of instruction and educational experience? Teaching, learning, and learning how to learn are related in at least these five ways.

A Spirit of Inquiry. Fostering a spirit of inquiry and curiosity enhances the learner, leaving behind positive residues in addition to the the information acquired. Activity that requires or encourages the learner to ask questions or identify or solve problems is relevant. Helping the learner sharpen his or her questions, for example, or internalize a problem-solving methodology would contribute even more. Teaching and learning activities aimed at seeing cause and effect, perceiving relationships, evaluating evidence together with guided practice in drawing inferences from data—these should make contributions toward the development of an inquiring mind.

The importance of such activities is emphasized by several writers who concern themselves with the process of learning how to learn, or learning about learning. Malcolm Knowles (1980b) speaks of the ability to formulate questions, based on one's curiosities, that are answerable through inquiry. Marilyn Ferguson (1980, p. 289) believes that "learning to see the relationship between things" and developing skill in asking "good" questions "lie at the heart of learning how to learn." One model of "essential life skills" equates knowledge of the problem-solving process with learning how to learn (McCoy 1980, p. 94). Inveighing against overemphasis on memorizing large amounts of factual material, Edgar Dale (1978) calls on the schools to teach students to read with questions in mind and in a questioning spirit. And Idries Shah (1978) points out that Sufi teachers sometimes provide deliberately contrived shocks to display the limitations of student thinking.

Critical thinking appears to be fostered through modeling, guided practice in reasoning, and opportunities to develop conceptual schemes for organizing information and solving problems. The conditions that favor inquiry include a safe environment and a certain amount of freedom. Critical thinking and a spirit of inquiry are also essential to learning to look analytically at education and learning themselves and coming to better understand oneself as a learner and one's learning processes.

Transference Capability.   The capacity to transfer has been called perhaps the most powerful capacity a person can possess (Selz and Ashley 1978). It involves the acquiring of instrumental habits that apply across teaching and learning situations and facilitate the mastery of new materials (Grover 1969). Jerome Bruner (1963) states that rigorous early schooling makes learning easier later—that one automatically learns to learn as one learns specifics. Bruner links transfer to problem solving when he calls it an example of generic skill in dealing with and recognizing a broad class of problems. He has contended that being able to apply concepts is an especially important learning skill.

Several generations back nearly all educators believed that studies in such disciplines as Latin, philosophy, law, and theology trained the mind by increasing learners' reasoning ability, memory, judgment, and attention. This view eventually gave way to regarding transfer as limited to situations containing elements matching those where application was to take place (training for desired outcomes), or to stressing the centrality of generalizing in the transfer process (helping students generalize from what is being learned by thinking through enough possible applications). The latter view presumes that learning takes place in a personally meaningful context (Lauffer 1978).

To the extent that the claims for the importance of the highly complex processes labeled transferring are sound, we can anticipate that learning-skill increments will accrue from learning that is perceived by the learner as having occurred, is regarded as relevant and worth applying, and is accompanied by "action images" of application (e.g., learners "picture" and "feel" themselves hitting a ball straight).

We can also anticipate that learning-skill increments will accrue from instruction that fosters the above outcomes and provides opportunities for learners to plan for application and implementation. (For example, concluding a workshop with a "back home" application session; or designing a workshop with three phases: theory presentation, application on the job, and a session for interpreting what happened when the theory was applied.)

Subject Matter Mastery. Regardless of the merits of one subject versus another, the study of a content area provides opportunity to learn to think critically and use the methods of inquiry peculiar to that subject. Indeed, the disciplines themselves can be regarded as systems for processing information and as bridges to meaningful experience—from the study of art history to the appreciation of art or from the study of psychology to self-understanding, for example. The application of a set of concepts is often involved. Thinking and reasoning are involved. Different ways of demonstrating proof and reaching conclusions are reflected in philosophy, history, and mathematics.

Assumptions come under review. Models and paradigms for showing relationships and classifying ideas are experienced. These can be helpful in the acquisition of a personal system for filing and retrieving information and past experience. If Alvin Toffler (1971) is right when he says learning how to learn includes knowing how and when to discard ideas and how and when to replace them, this ability may be fostered by the direct experience of the evolution that a discipline undergoes with regard to its content and methods of inquiry—by studying the history of a science, for example. Students can come to understand that knowledge is constantly being restructured as well as added to (Ferguson 1980).

Instruction in a subject area stands to strengthen people as learners to the extent that it is free from pedantry and retains freshness. Instructors who themselves model active learning behavior and constantly question the very foundations of their own life's work are helping students learn to examine their assumptions, retain their natural curiosity, and search for new meanings.

Learning how to learn presumably can also be enhanced through the fashioning of subject matter instruction to equip students to proceed toward higher levels of achievement after the termination of course work. Foreign language instruction is the ideal example. Instruction resulting in the following outcomes has proved to foster the postcourse learning required for mastery of a language: an awareness of units of language description, the ability to make decisions concerning the organization of language materials, and the ability to correct oneself (Dickinson and Carver 1980).

Self-Understanding. Educational experience that involves constructive self-examination stands to leave the learner better equipped for further learning because a central task of learning how to learn is developing awareness of oneself as learner. Therapy and instruction in human relations are frequently directed toward self-understanding. But one need not be a therapist or small-group facilitator to further this outcome in others. It might be furthered through such activities as direct artistic expression and responding to art (music, literature, film, architecture, drama, painting, sculpture), writing autobiographical essays, or keeping a diary. It might also be furthered by helping students relate problems, issues, and ideas to their own lives and by helping them to acquire new ways of perceiving their environment. Instruction that encourages fuller utilization of the senses and "both halves" of the brain is presumed by some to encourage such effects (McCarthy 1980; Roberts 1975).

Process Awareness. Self-understanding links directly to learning how to learn when learners become sensitive to, and in control of, the learning processes, in other words, more aware of themselves as learners.

> Learning how to learn involves a set of processes in which the individual learner acts at least partially as his own manager of change, and his focus of change is his own self-concept and learning processes. This requires that the learner be able to conceptualize his own learning process and be able to pay some attention to how he goes about learning . . . [and] trust himself to manage this process. (Brundage and MacKeracher 1980, p. 30)

Or again, as Laurie Thomas and Sheila Harri-Augstein (1977) put it, "Awareness of one's own processes in learning is . . . a prerequisite for learning to learn."

Anything that happens in a learning episode or an educational situation that fosters these processes and related skills contributes to learning how to learn. Anything that contributes to one's understanding of what helps or hinders his or her learning stands to contribute, whether or not it's done deliberately and intentionally for these purposes. It may be done unconsciously when one reflects on an experience (processes it) or consciously when, for example, instructors provide feedback concerning the how of learning as well as the what (what was learned about process as well as content).

Donald Maudsley uses the term *meta-learning* to refer to the process by which learners become aware of and take increased control over previously internalized processes of perception, inquiry, learning, and growth. Synthesizing five existing theories, he suggests that meta-learning comes about when people examine their habitual ways of interacting with the world (their "rules") and underlying assumptions ("fixed ideas about what the world is like"), and then "reorganize" themselves—change their rules and assumptions as a result of new information introduced from the environment. An example of an assumption would be that one can no longer learn. The kind of educational practices and conditions that enhance possibilities for meta-learning to transpire are those that maximize learners' options and responsibility for learning, and allow learners to "find their own directions" in learning situations. The facilitation of meta-learning (read "training") requires a theory, however primitive. The process often involves discomfort and often culminates in a sudden insight followed by a sense of relief and well-being (Maudsley 1979).

Bruce Joyce (1981) envisions ideal schooling that systematically introduces people to an ever wider repertoire of approaches to learning. As we saw earlier in this chapter, optimum conditions for adult learning include the availability of multiple options and maximum feasible utilization of learners themselves as resources for learning and as directors of their own learning by their sharing in program development. Educational activities implemented under these conditions would "automatically" leave the person concerned better equipped and motivated for further learning.

> The adult education program which gives top priority to the individual, actively involves him in the educational experience and provides him with useful feedback will be helping him learn how to learn. (Jensen 1970, p. 519)

We see then that learning itself intersects learning how to learn because, as we learn, things happen that affect our motivation for further learning and our potential for learning more efficiently, effectively, and meaningfully. The chances that positive and desirable learning related to learning itself will accrue from educational (as opposed to training) experience increase to the extent that the experience fosters an inquiring mind and openness to change, and results in understanding of self, especially of self as learner, and of learning's processes. These residual effects of educational activity are most likely to accrue when educators take into account the characteristics of adult learners and the conditions under which they learn best, pay attention to how learning occurs as well as to what is being taught, encourage application of what is learned, and employ established subject matter areas as gateways to understanding the nature and potential of knowledge itself and for acquiring the skills of inquiry. Fortunate indeed are the adults whose early years were filled with education of this kind. They should require relatively little training in order to learn effectively as adults.

In this chapter I have described some characteristics of adult learners and some optimum learning conditions that appear to be central to learning how to learn. The relationship between learning (and teaching) and learning how to learn was explored. Chapter 3 now takes up learning style, another element of the learning how to learn construct.

3

Learning Style

*"Everything, men, animals, trees, stars, we are all one
substance involved in the same terrible struggle. What
struggle? . . . Turning matter into spirit."*
 *Zorba scratched his head [and said] "I've got a thick
skull boss, I don't grasp these things easily. Ah, if only you
could dance all that you've just said, then I'd
understand. . . . Or if you could tell me all that in a story,
boss."*

Nikos Kazantzakis
Zorba the Greek

The hero of Kazantzakis's fine novel reveals some clear personal preferences for trying to understand new information. Viewing and listening are both acceptable to him, but he prefers to have abstractions
made concrete and ideas presented through action. Like most adults,
Zorba has insight into his own learning style.

In chapter 1 learning style was introduced and defined as people's
characteristic ways of information processing, feeling, and behaving in
and toward learning situations—in other words, those preferences, dispositions, and tendencies that influence one's learning. It was mentioned that adults differ as to how they go about thinking and solving
problems as well as in their preferences for methods, environments,
and structure. Also explored was the relationship of learning style to
the two other components, or subconcepts, of the learning how to learn
concept: needs (what people need to know and be able to do for success
in learning) and training (organized activity directed toward increasing competencies in learning). Knowledge of learning style was termed
useful in becoming an effective adult learner and an effective adult
educator.

This chapter sets forth some of the theoretical bases of explanation
of the learning style concept together with suggestions for applications
by administrators, programmers, instructors, counselors, and adult
learners. It begins with an examination of the three major components

of style: the individualized cognitive, affective, and environmental factors that impinge on learning.

Cognitive Factors

When we go about activities such as working, playing, and learning, we use our minds and our senses in consistent ways. We have acquired preferred patterns of perceiving, remembering, thinking, and problem solving. Complex cognitive strategies, structures, and controls are at work that enable us to deal successfully with the myriad stimuli that come our way. They permit us to conceptually organize our environment, they help pattern our behavior, and they constitute a major component of learning style.

Field-Independence versus Field-Dependence. Long-term research by the late Herman Witkin and his associates demonstrated the usefulness of placing people on a continuum with regard to the extent of their tendencies to perceive the environment in an analytical (field-independent) as opposed to a global (field-dependent) way. Witkin found cognitive style to be a potent factor in academic choices and success, vocational preferences, and how students learn and interact with teachers.

As the name implies, the field-independent person tends to perceive elements independently of context or background. The elements are not restricted to the visual—they can include a tune embedded in a complex melody or a simple figure embedded in a complex figure with raised contours. The field-dependent person tends to deal with a total field or situation encountered. The field-independent individual approaches situations in an analytical way, separating elements from their background. Tending to see the whole rather than the parts, the field-dependent person approaches things in a global way.

The most commonly used instrument to assess people's tendency toward field-dependence or field-independence is the Embedded Figures Test. (Most of the inventories mentioned in this chapter are summarized in Appendix A.) It employs superimposed designs like the following:

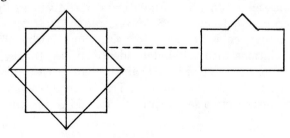

Field-dependence is indicated by difficulty in locating the diagram at the right when it is hidden in the more complex context on the left.

In learning situations, field-dependents prefer relatively greater amounts of external structure, direction, and feedback. They tend to be comfortable with learning and problem solving through collaboration, reaching consensus faster than field-independents in discussion groups. When problem solving involves analysis, field-dependents are not at their best. Applying rules, and perhaps intuiting, suits them better.

Field-independence is associated with a more internally directed approach to learning requiring less external structure and feedback. Field-independents are believed to be less influenced by the rewards of their social surroundings and less influenced by peers. They tend to be better than field-dependents at analytical problem solving, while at a disadvantage in collaborative learning. They accommodate well to abstraction and have relatively high need for achievement (Cross 1976; Kirby 1979; Kogan 1971).

Conceptualizing and Categorizing. People demonstrate consistency in how they form and use concepts in interpreting information, thinking, and problem-solving. Jerome Kagan has led the research in this area. Relational-contextual categorizing (to use his terminology) involves a tendency to use concepts of functional or thematic similarity. Bits of information are made to go together. Analytical-descriptive conceptualizing involves finding similarity in things based on the external, objective, physical attributes of stimuli and information. Analytical-descriptives use external categories in which the self does not play as central a role as it does with relational-contextuals. Confronted with three items—meat, cheese, and bread, for example—the relational-contextual person (also called global) might describe them as a sandwich, while the analytical-descriptive person might call them edibles (Kirby 1979).

These bases for conceptualizing appear to be developmentally ordered. The relational is associated with children, the analytical with adulthood. However, since the relational-contextual dimension seems to correlate positively with creativity, it should not be regarded as primitive (Messick et al. 1976). Analytical-descriptives are "generally faster at learning analytical types of concepts . . . and good at disregarding what they feel is irrelevant to a situation" (Kirby 1979, p. 57). Possible correlations with field-independence suggest themselves.

One instrument developed by Kagan to identify these dispositions and tendencies is the Conceptual Style Test. It requires individuals to select two pictures from a set of three that could go together. Analytical-descriptives group pictures on a basis of common elements, such as people without shoes, while relational-contextuals use functional, thematic patterns in their groupings.

Kolb and Fry developed a model of the learning cycle itself that integrated conceptualizing tendencies. Learning is portrayed as a cyclical process with four kinds of activities. The learner can begin with any of the four and proceed through the cycle. For fully integrated learning to occur, all activities must eventually be utilized. Style is seen as two-dimensional. The dimension on the vertical axis relates to conceptualizing processes, which range from concrete to abstract. On the horizontal axis cognitive manipulations, ranging from active to reflective (or symbolic) are represented (Kolb and Fry 1975).

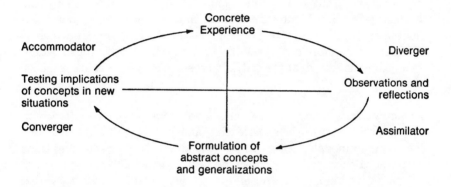

Kolb developed a self-assessment instrument, the Learning Styles Inventory, to explore individual tendencies related to this theory. It measures how an individual learns from experience, or adapts, by the rank ordering of nine sets of four words in terms of the degree to which a word best characterizes that individual's learning style (an example set: intuitive, productive, logical, questioning). The instrument yields a profile, or grid, that permits classifying people as accommodators, divergers, convergers, or assimilators.

These ways of looking at perceiving, conceptualizing, and categorizing—and a dozen others found in the literature—involve such complex and interrelated dimensions and processes that one longs for a simplifying construct, perhaps even an oversimplifying one. The "splitter-lumper" distinction has been suggested as a response to the question, Does the person look at reality by splitting it apart into small pieces or by lumping it together into a big picture? Proposed by R. A. Cohen, the distinction seems to have potential for practical applications of psychological research to learning and to style diagnosis. "Lumpers" take their cue from the immediate environment, are "reactive" (rather than "proactive"), and can be viewed as carrying a radarlike potential into each situation. "Splitters" are guided on a preset course as by a gyroscope; they are more internally directed and more "proactive" (Kirby 1979).

Reflectivity versus Impulsivity. Objectified on this dimension are differences in the speed and adequacy with which alternative hypotheses are formed and information processed. In learning situations requiring correct answers, impulsive individuals often tend to give the answer that occurs to them immediately or relatively quickly, while reflective individuals consider more possibilities more carefully before responding. This dimension is roughly analogous to risk taking and cautiousness. Reflectivity and impulsivity can be measured by the Matching Familiar Figures Test, in which the subject is shown a familiar object together with eight similar stimuli, only one of which is identical to the standard; the subject is asked to identify the one identical stimulus and is appraised in terms of accuracy versus response time.

Sensory Modalities. These pertain to people's relative reliance on the respective senses in experiencing and in organizing information. Three major modalities are utilized: the kinesthetic (or enactive) leads to physical or motoric thinking, the visual (or ikonic) leads to figural or spatial thinking, and the auditory (or symbolic) leads to verbal thinking. Although all three sensory modalities can function in parallel with information from one clarifying and implementing information from the other two, individuals differ markedly in their preferred reliance on one or the other of these means of representation thus resulting in characteristic differences in learning and thinking styles (Messick et al. 1976). Another quality, especially relevant to younger people's learning, is labeled tactual—the need or ability to learn through touching.

The complex system of learning style mapping developed by the late Joseph Hill and his associates includes batteries of tests to determine how people create and use symbols, including sensory symbols, to derive meaning from their environment and acquire knowledge. Included in the resulting personal map, or profile, is the ability to acquire meaning through hearing, smelling, tasting, touching, and seeing.

We have mentioned a few of the cognitive dimensions of style identified by psychologists. There is a tendency for most of these constructs to share the following characteristics, despite variations in the amount of empirical research upon which they rest and the degree of methodological refinement for their assessment: (1) a concern with the process of cognition, (2) a tendency to cross domains of function or ability, and (3) a bipolarity, with each pole having adaptive value in different spheres or situations (Messick et al. 1976).

Affective Considerations

Structure and Authority. The amount of structure and authority the learner prefers, or most profits from, varies from person to person and, to complicate matters, from situation to situation. Structure has to do with the imposition of rules, guidelines, and prescriptions for carrying out learning activities. It limits the number of options available to learners and imposes ways of seeking information, responding, and demonstrating achievement. In formal education settings it comes largely from the instructor. When people learn on their own or in the collaborative mode, the choices they make about such matters as objectives, responses, strategies, and pace of learning bring structure into being.

It was brought out in chapter 2 that the current pressures toward so-called self-directed learning and fostering self-directed learners are well intentioned and potentially useful but also simplistic. It was pointed out (1) that interdependence and even dependence can be as functional as independence and autonomy, (2) that different modes of learning require differing degrees of autonomy, and (3) that there is potential danger in confronting learners with the responsibility for exercising more autonomy than experience or training have prepared them to exercise.

Need for authority and authoritarianism have been the subject of much research by behavioral and social scientists. The authoritarian personality has been advanced as a basic type, with characteristic patterns of thinking and behaving. This person tends to think in terms of stereotypes and rigid categories and to accept overly simplistic explanations. Rigidity and intolerance of ambiguity have been found in manifestations of learning style (Goldstein and Blackman 1978). Intolerance versus tolerance for unrealistic (i.e., not readily verifiable) experience is a related characteristic or tendency. Messick describes the range of the latter dimension and ways of measuring it:

> The tolerant pole of the dimension reflects a predisposition to accept and report events and ideas which are markedly different from the ordinary, while the intolerant extreme implies a tendency to remain closely oriented to reality and to prefer conventional ideas. Persons tolerant of unrealistic experi-

ences, for example, tend more than their intolerant peers to
report wider ranges of apparent movement when exposed to
flashing lights, more rapid reversals when viewing reversible
figures, more form-labile responses on the Rorschach [test],
and more and longer associations on word-association tests.
(Messick et al. 1976, p. 20)

A few studies related to these matters are of interest. One found
that adults participating in noncredit courses had strongest preferences for control of educational planning related to the setting of overall course goals and that those who were studying issues desired more
control than those who were learning skills (Humphrey 1974). Adults
engaged in personal learning projects have been found to vary consid-
erably in how much help from others they tend to use, and individuals
vary the amount of external help from project to project (Tough 1979).
A study of 2,800 community-college students found those over twenty-
five years of age preferred more structure than their younger counter-
parts (Ommen et al. 1979). And, in a study of the learning styles of
college students studying physical therapy in forty-two separate programs, the typical student was found to prefer a relatively high
amount of course organization and structure (Payton et al. 1979).

Several instruments and strategies for appraising adult learning
style explore learner preferences for autonomy and structure. Five of
the twenty-one indices on the Canfield Learning Style Inventory
(CLS), an earlier version of which was used in the Ommen and the
Payton studies, pertain to these concerns, as do three of the twenty-
one indices on the Productivity Environmental Preference Survey
(PEPS). The Paragraph Completion Method, in which people write
short responses to topics such as "What I Think About Rules," is
designed to assess how much structure the individual requires for optimum learning (Hunt et al. 1978). Shutz's FIRO-B assesses need for
control. Finally, an inventory devoted entirely to ascertaining the extent of people's capability for exercising autonomy in learning has
been developed by Lucy Guglielmino. Called the Self-directed Learning Readiness Scale, the instrument asks the individual to read a statement (for example, "It's really up to me to learn—the school and the
teachers can't do it for me") and indicate the degree to which that
statement is an accurate self-description.

How can the need for authority, autonomy, and structure in adult
education be represented and analyzed? Difficulties arise because people's response to and need for autonomy and structure in education
and learning will not plot readily along a single dimension. The factors
involved include a variety of linked but discrete activities like goal

setting, resource selection, instructional techniques, and means of getting feedback and assessing progress.

As a way to classify education programs according to the amount of learner autonomy exercised, a twenty-four-celled grid has been proposed by Michael Moore (1972, p. 82). Moore's approach derives from the fact that in the most simple terms, an undertaking like a learning project, a course, or even a single class session has three major activities to be carried out: preparation, execution, and evaluation. It is planned, conducted, and evaluated. Programs can be plotted on a grid that places those permitting the learner to exercise a great deal of autonomy over all three functions at one extreme (Type 1) and those permitting very little learner autonomy in any of the three (Type 8) at the other extreme.

	Preparation	*Execution*	*Evaluation*
1.	A	A	A
2.	A	A	N
3.	A	N	A
4.	A	N	N
5.	N	A	A
6.	N	N	A
7.	N	A	N
8.	N	N	N

A = Autonomous
N = Non-Autonomous

In addition to providing a way to classify programs according to the nature and degree of self-direction they entail, this typology suggests a way to look at individual preferences for control of the respective phases in an educational endeavor. One might prefer (and therefore seek or be directed toward) programs that emphasize the degree of autonomy found in any of the respective combinations.

From experience and the limited research available we can suggest some implications concerning control and autonomy in the three basic modes of learning. In the self-directed mode, persons conducting personal learning projects will retain nominal control throughout their projects. But the degree of autonomy exercised at various stages (planning, conducting, and evaluating) and processes (e.g., goal setting or using a resource) will vary from person to person and from learning project to learning project. This mode will obviously require the most autonomy of the three for effective learning.

In the collaborative mode, as in self-directed learning, individuals will retain nominal control of the overall progress of the venture. At times they will almost certainly bring in outside resources (e.g., an expert) and temporarily relinquish varying amounts of control depending on the choice and use made of those resources. At other times, members will need to do some outside inquiry on their own if learning is to be most effective. This mode will require a moderate amount of autonomy on the part of the individual.

In the traditional mode, because the individual enrolls in a formal activity provided by an educational agency, he or she usually expects the locus of control to reside with the provider. It is the educational agency's responsibility, for which it can be held accountable, to provide overall direction and structure to ensure that the specified or implied educational purposes are fulfilled, though only the individual participant can ensure that learning actually transpires. Although this mode usually requires less autonomy than the self-directed and the collaborative, individuals need to exercise varying amounts of autonomy because educational agents (usually instructors) can exercise wide variations in the amount of designated authority relinquished to them by the institution. The amount of authority the instructor exercises tends to be affected by (1) the subject matter characteristics, (2) the learning purposes and tasks, (3) the learners' readiness to assume control or responsibility, (4) the availability of training to enable learners to assume greater control of decisions and responsibilities affecting learning and instruction, and (5) the personality of the instructor.

Expectations and Motivation. While some variation can be expected from situation to situation, learners usually exhibit consistency in the energy and zest with which they go forth to educational settings and participate in learning activities.

We can compare the learner to the athlete, though the analogy should not be pressed too far. Some athletes almost always play with intensity and determination, requiring little urging from coaches or crowds. They expect to win and seem never to give up. At the other extreme are those whose performance is uneven and who often appear subject to doubt and discouragement; coaches search for those with the so-called winning attitude and strive to develop it in those they lead. When confronted with a learning task that proves difficult, people vary in the length of time they will persist in the effort to accomplish it. Some lose interest quickly, perhaps becoming irritated and temporarily withdrawing or even abandoning the effort altogether. ("Avoidant" is one of the six styles yielded by the Grasha-Riechmann questionnaire.) Adults can develop strategies for minimizing the negative effect of this tendency when diagnosis reveals its presence; skillful instructors seek to revive flagging motivation by varying resources, activities, and pace of learning for individuals and subgroups with differing levels of persistence and differing attention spans.

It has been well documented that expectation of success plays an important role in learning. If a schoolteacher expects a pupil to do well, the pupil tends to do so (and the teacher often sees that he or she does so). More important for adult learning—most of which is voluntary and much of which is at least nominally self-directed—is the degree to which one undertakes learning activities and problem-solving tasks with a positive attitude toward the desired outcome and with realistic expectations. Some people have learned to set demanding yet realistic goals for themselves. Others have not, either greatly underestimating or overestimating what they can accomplish.

Self-perception concerning attitude toward learning is explored in several instruments. The PEPS produces a "motivated-unmotivated" and a "persistence" descriptor on the individual's profile (for example, "I usually finish what I start."). "Expectation" is a major phase of the CLS and is defined as level of anticipated performance (for example, "Do you usually expect a superior, good, average, or poor grade on a paper submitted to an instructor?"). Clayton Lafferty's "Life Styles Inventory," a measure of twelve basic styles of behavior, includes an "achievement style," which represents maximum concern for "task completion" and a tendency to gain high reward from achievement for its own sake. (Achievement motivation has its theoretical base in the long-term research of David McClelland and his associates, first reported in 1953 in *The Achievement Motive.)*

Degree of Interest in Subject Matter.   Expectation and motivation are affected by one's reaction toward the subject or skill to be learned. Previous experience in schooling with the same or a similar subject can strongly shape that reaction. For this reason efforts to diagnose learning style may include assessing the individual's preferred areas of interest. The CLS seeks to find out if a person has greatest interest when the subject matter or task involves working with numbers and logic, words and language, inanimate objects, or people.

Environmental Factors

This component of learning style includes considerations that range from such a specific matter as preferred room temperature to the amount of affiliation and emotional support learners find helpful in the immediate environment.

People vary in the amount of light they prefer when learning. Observing them in their homes will easily verify this. Anyone who has attended or conducted a workshop knows that it is not easy to get everyone in a room to agree that the temperature is right, the chairs suitable, or the walls appropriately colored. Another consideration is sound level, especially how much external sound one can tolerate or block out when trying to learn. When studying, or carrying out other activities related to learning, some people actually prefer music or similar background sound to silence, others are distracted by external sound, while still others can accommodate to either condition.

Light is a factor that appears to affect fewer people than does sound, though a small percentage of people have quite negative reactions to strong lighting. For others bright light seems to serve as an energizer. Some people find it difficult to concentrate when seated on anything but a straight-backed chair at a table or desk. For others such physical surroundings appear to suppress motivation and creativity. People also differ with regard to preference for mobility—opportunities to stand and move about—while learning (NASSP 1979).

While technically not an environmental consideration, preferred time of day is frequently included here. Rita Dunn (1979) has developed a fifteen-item questionnaire for self-assessment of preferred time of day for learning.

People differ in the extent to which they prefer an informal and supportive climate as opposed to a more formal and impersonal one. Some learning environments are characterized by a high degree of expressed interpersonal concern. Those responsible seek to develop a warm, friendly atmosphere. Feedback to learners often stresses what they are doing right rather than their errors. The expression of feelings is encouraged. The educator and the learner may be on a first-name basis. Learners may be encouraged to help one another. (One early definition of adult education was "friends learning from each other.")

To this we can hypothetically oppose a climate that is much more formal and impersonal. Here feedback may center on the errors made. The expression of feelings may never become normative: instructors and resource persons will tend to keep their distance from learners. Competition often supplants collaboration. While some learners can be at home in either climate, most apparently gravitate toward one climate or the other.

Adult learning style inventories that take environmental conditions into consideration include the CLS and the PEPS. The CLS profiles desire for working with others, for competition, for supportive relationships, and for knowing the instructor personally; the PEPS puts considerable emphasis on reaction to the immediate physical environment and preferred time of day for learning. The Grasha-Riechmann Student Learning Styles Questionnaire, oriented to the style of students in college classes, enables an instructor to differentiate students who prefer collaboration from those who prefer competition. For a summary of some learning-style inventories, see Appendix A.

Matching and Changing Styles

The question arises as to the desirability of always seeking to effect a match between educational treatment and learners' characteristic styles. While a prolonged mismatch is clearly undesirable, some educators feel a responsibility to expose learners for short periods to instructors, approaches, environments, and methodologies that are not in line with learners' preferences and strengths. Some feel that this will help people to accommodate to situations in which they have no choice but to accommodate (i.e., to develop flexibility); there is evidence that higher levels of learning style flexibility accompany higher achievement levels (Kirby 1979). Others feel that deliberate mismatching may help to foster creativity in learning and problem solving.

Many writers maintain that failure to factor style into the teaching-learning equation has been a major weakness in education: ". . . the quality and durability of learning are critically dependent upon whether the teaching strategy is matched to the individual [style]" (Hamkins 1974). For example, a multiple-choice test may well give an advantage to persons who prefer broad categories of response and tend to respond with quick, insightful approximations in answering a test item over those who prefer a narrow range of categories for response and tend to search carefully for exact solutions (Kirby 1979). The schools have been called places where "convergent" thinkers are rewarded while "divergent" thinkers are disapproved and suppressed for tendencies to pursue their own problems or approach them in idiosyncratic ways (Moore 1972). "Our schools are structures for analytic learners" (McCarthy 1980). And it has been suggested that instruction in higher education has favored the field-independent (Cross 1976).

An in-depth review of the research finds some instructional variation to be "distinctly bad for a fraction of the learners" with "some treatments benefiting one subgroup while producing negative effects for another" (Cronbach and Snow 1977, p. 391). Describing the great effort by schools to improve instruction by individualizing it, one publication sums up the position of those who feel that style can no longer be ignored.

These efforts ranged from programed learning to flexible scheduling, and from computer-assisted instruction to interactive television. While these programs—and others—enjoyed some success, the general reaction among most practitioners was one of disappointment. No one model appeared to be superior. Student achievement tended to remain constant whether schooling was structured or unstructured. Student attitudes and motivation blew hot and cold depending on the approach.

With the benefit of hindsight, we now see that part of the problem was the tendency to apply a single approach to all students. That is, all students were expected to blossom under independent study or small-group discussion or open classrooms, or whatever. Student learning style challenges this premise and argues for an eclectic instructional program, one based upon a variety of techniques and structures reflecting the different ways that individual students acquire knowledge and skill. (NASSP 1979, p. i)

In elementary, secondary, and higher education positive results from learning style applications are being reported with mounting frequency. *Student Learning Styles* contains numerous examples and states that two studies have demonstrated significant academic gains (NASSP 1979, p. 54). Undergraduate physical therapy students forced to learn in their least preferred ways experienced higher anxiety levels and more negative attitudes toward the instruction than a comparable group that learned in their most preferred ways (Payton et al. 1979). After a learning style inventory was given to dental hygiene students, Shuntich and Kirkhorn (1979) found that both the students and their instructors were able to use the information generated and that increased student motivation resulted.

With adults, examples of the consequences of failure to take learning style into account come from several recent studies. One involved 206 people preparing to take the General Education Development (GED) test of high school equivalency. The study revealed that the field-dependent person is apparently at a disadvantage in taking this important exam despite the fact that more field-dependents than field-independents take it (Loveall 1979). Another produced findings that prompted the investigators to say that those preparing learners for the GED test may well be conducting an educational experience that is difficult and frustrating for the field-dependent learner (Donnarumma et al. 1980). And, observing English as a Second Language classes composed of Laotian students, Lert found that cross-cultural insensitivity to learning style was apparently responsible for the students' lack of progress:

I observed an atmosphere of tension and disorientation in the classroom which . . . I felt to be symptomatic of a cultural clash . . . [resulting from] a lack of awareness Anglo teachers and administrators had regarding the students' preferred learning techniques. These included mimesis, identification with teacher, peer communication, and group cooperation and support. (Lert 1980, p. 58)

Thus we have seen that a rapidly growing body of instruments for diagnosing learning styles is now available and in use for instructional, investigative, and training purposes. Educational institutions are mobilizing to take style into account, and training for style applications is increasingly common.

Some Practical Applications of Learning Style

Style theory and instrumentation offer an educational agency two options. The chief decision-makers (e.g., deans, directors, principals) can choose to make a sustained effort to encourage applications of existing knowledge about style by program developers, instructors, resource persons, and counselors; or they can leave the matter to the initiative of persons in these roles. When senior administrators take the latter course, individual adult educators obviously can choose to ignore the style factor; or they can make efforts to put it to work in program development, instruction, or counseling. The consumers of adult education services, and persons who direct their own education, also have the option of seeking to use knowledge of style to their advantage. Thus application of style can then be looked at from the point of view of the administrator or program developer, the instructor and counselor, and the individual adult learner.

Administrative and Programmatic Applications. The principal of Highland High in Bakersfield, California, led a comprehensive effort to apply learning style in that school. After reviewing literature on style, he instituted a seven-member faculty study and implementation committee. The committee members developed an instrument to get at students' environmental preferences. They used the Embedded Figures Test and the People in Society Scale to assess field sensitiveness and the locus of control factor. Eight English teachers conducted an experiment involving the tenth-grade class to study relationships between a student's choice of learning environment ("open," "hybrid," "traditional") and his or her cognitive style. This long-term project left the administration convinced that "matching students with selected learning environments is an efficacious way of increasing student achievement" (NASSP 1979, p. 88).

At Fox Valley (Wisconsin) Technical Institute a system-wide effort was undertaken to identify learning styles relevant to vocational-technical education, to develop an individualized learning model, and to construct alternative learning experiences for meeting a given objective. A "Learning Activities Questionnaire" was developed (to get at the "concrete/symbolic" and "structured/unstructured" style dimensions) and made available to teachers for learning-style diagnosis and "individualizing a program, a course, or an activity" (Oen 1973).

The best known and most comprehensive effort by a senior administrator to apply style theory is that of Joseph Hill, the late president of Oakland (Michigan) Community College (Hill 1981). Over more than a decade, Hill undertook a variety of activities to improve instruction by taking learning style and teaching style into account. Under his leadership an entire system for testing and style mapping of incoming students was developed and linked to various diagnostic, counseling, and instructional processes. As mentioned earlier, Hill announced significant positive results, and his system, which has received its share of criticism (Sherriff 1977), proved successful enough to trigger its use in and adaptation to a number of other colleges and secondary schools. Instruments and mapping procedures growing out of Hill's work are now presented in training workshops throughout the country. Patricia Kirby (1979) presents a balanced appraisal of the Oakland College experiment and Hill's work.

Projects of this kind suggest several possibilities for administrators who decide to take style into account and move toward implementation. Administrators can establish or encourage in-service education for themselves and their staffs concerning learning-style theory and application and obtain information about training opportunities from sources mentioned in Appendix A. Or administrators can assemble a set of style inventories for their staffs to examine and try out. They can also set up task forces to explore possible applications of style in the agencies. In addition, they can install learning-style diagnosis as a regular intake or new-student orientation procedure making individual profiles available to faculties, staffs, and students. Finally, they can budget monies for style-related activities as testimony to the fact that the commitment is real.

Programming Applications. When individuals or groups design a curriculum, a course, or a workshop, they make decisions about audience (learners), goals, subject matter, and methodology. They seek to bring about educational situations and learning experiences that will meet certain needs, interests, and objectives in an effective and economical way. Especially with adults, they have to take into account a wide variety of variables and details—from overall program philosophy (e.g., how much learner involvement in planning to incorporate) to room arrangements and availability of audio-visual equipment.

Although some program-planning models have as many as thirty steps, the basic components they most often account for are participant needs and interests, goals, learning resources, procedures and strategies (e.g., lecture, discussion, keeping a log, interviewing a resource person), and evaluation.

These elements often appear in program-planning models in a linear or steplike fashion. For example:

1. Determine needs and interests.
2. Set goals and evaluative criteria.
3. Identify promising resources and procedures.
4. Select program format and activities.
5. Conduct program.
6. Evaluate and follow-up.

Sometimes, to encourage using a cyclical approach in which evaluation and follow-up yield new needs for the next round of programming, these elements appear in a circular fashion.

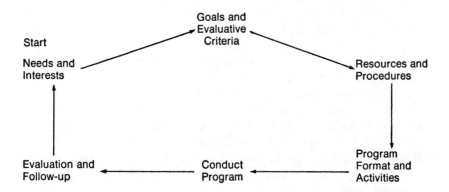

Programmers now have an opportunity to insert learning style into the planning process. They have always been urged to carefully examine their intended audience or clientele. Careful programmers have usually sought to reflect on the potential participants' age, experience, and knowledge of what is to be learned before making decisions about content and procedures. But style diagnosis provides a way to include an even more significant thing to know about those whom the program is designed to help learn: how they apparently learn best. Examination of the inherent characteristics of methods and materials provides a potentially firmer basis for making decisions about learning activities and for setting appropriate objectives. The new programming model should therefore probably look something like this.

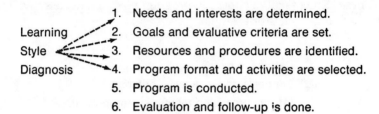

Learning
Style
Diagnosis

1. Needs and interests are determined.
2. Goals and evaluative criteria are set.
3. Resources and procedures are identified.
4. Program format and activities are selected.
5. Program is conducted.
6. Evaluation and follow-up is done.

The point at which learning-style diagnosis enters the process cannot be definitely prescribed (hence the dotted arrows) because it will be affected by such factors as whether one is programming from the outset for a predetermined clientele or finding out later who the participants will be. The preferable position would be prior to step 3.

Persons planning a workshop for, say, health professionals thus might present learners with parallel sets of activities, one rather highly structured and didactic, the other less structured and more affiliative. The use of a learning-style inventory would make possible such programmatic decisions and provide a way for each participant to make a choice as to which track to follow.

Program planners should consider some style-related questions like these: What program-development model are we using? What major components does it have? Where and how can we fit into it the results of learning-style diagnosis? What style-assessment inventory or inventories will be appropriate for our purposes? Are there special problems in using style diagnosis with our clients? How can they be coped with? Who will carry out the diagnostic process, and how can the information gathered be presented, in a manner that will be useful for making planning decisions?

Instructional and Counseling Applications. Adult learners in institutional settings usually rely on a program coordinator or an instructor for guidance and counseling, since few programs can afford a counseling staff and few people are professionally prepared for the educational counseling of adults. Whatever the source of advice and support, knowledge of learning style provides a framework and tool for counseling to help people find appropriate instruction, profit from that instruction, and participate until personal goals are achieved.

Style inventories and style-related diagnostic questions can be used for placement purposes or for diagnosing causes of difficulty and forestalling drop out. A better fit between instructor and student can often result. When multiple program options are available, learning-style diagnosis provides a basis for helping the student make an appropriate choice—for example, deciding between a curriculum requiring a great deal of self-direction and one that provides a considerable amount of structure.

Instructors of adults can use learning-style inventories to get a perspective on how they themselves prefer to learn. They can monitor their teaching for signs of the same tendencies McCarthy (1980) found in elementary and secondary schoolteachers: to teach the way they themselves prefer to learn.

Instructors can use learning-style inventories to gather information for making decisions about teaching and helping people learn. The decisions may concern materials selection, presentation of information, individualizing, and subgrouping of students as well as evaluative procedures. Since every learner is unique and every class has a different mix, style inventories represent a tool for looking more clearly at one's objectives and procedures in relation to the specific clients at hand.

A professor of adult education has described how the Kolb's Learning Style Inventory helped her to solve instructional problems in a graduate course, one in which students tended to possess a diverse set of preferences on how to structure their time together. The preferences seemed to grow out of different definitions of what learning is and of what her role as a teacher should be. She reported that administering and discussing the Learning Style Inventory surfaced the differences early in the course and led to a better teacher-student understanding and more active efforts to learn than previous participants in the course had shown (Griffin 1979).

Instructors can diagnose learning style without ready-made inventories. They can adapt existing ones or devise their own. Merely observing people, listening to them, and asking them questions about how they prefer to learn and undergo evaluation can yield useful information. However, a commercially available inventory can provide a useful framework for informal diagnosis.

Some pertinent questions about perceiving and processing information could be, What kind of activities does the learner respond to with interest or handle best? Does the learner seem to get the most from reading, reading and listening, listening only, or an activity such as simulation and role play? Is the learner's choice of words more visual or action oriented? Does the learner tend to define things in abstract or concrete terms? Does the learner try to see the "big picture" first or does he or she begin working in a narrower, more linear fashion?

Pertinent questions about environment, structure, and motivation could be, When and where does the learner prefer to learn? How much structure, direct feedback, and support seem needed? How does the learner respond to learning with peers?

Instructors and counselors of adults can involve learners in style diagnosis by putting such questions to them and by sharing with them the results when style inventories are administered. The secure instructor can share information concerning his or her own learning and teaching preferences in an effort to get the best fit with learners and help them to make wider applications of insights into preferred learning style. Finally, instructors should bear in mind that style diagnosis—like teaching itself—remains an art, and that no amount of instrumentation will compensate for faulty interpretation of the information available.

To summarize, when diagnosing, (1) use, adapt, or devise one or more instruments; (2) ask questions and observe; (3) try to avoid jumping to conclusions or an overly simplistic diagnosis; (4) share tentative conclusions with the learner, making adjustments as they seem warranted; and (5) reflect on the implications for instruction, learning, and the individual's better understanding of himself or herself as a learner.

Application by Individual Adult Learners. The more one understands the self as learner, the better equipped one is to learn and to take advantage of the myriad educational offerings that are now available. The learning-style concept represents one potential bridge and gateway to such understanding.

The individual adult can move toward insights into himself or herself as a learner by seeking out training opportunities in which learning style is explored. Training is likely to focus on a single approach to style theory, instrumentation, diagnosis, and application. Workshops conducted by Rita and Kenneth Dunn, Bernice McCarthy, Albert Canfield, and proponents of the Myers-Briggs approach and of Hill's cognitive-style mapping are examples. Public programming agencies (e.g., colleges) can also be encouraged to conduct training activities.

More modestly, individuals can obtain one or more of the learning-style inventories summarized in Appendix A. Most of these inventories can be filled out and sent in for scoring. The resulting profile or profiles can serve as a basis for self-analysis and can be discussed with others. Or the inventory can be used merely as a trigger for reflection and personal insight.

It is well to keep in mind that the learning-style concept and the results yielded by inventories are trends and rough approximations. There is not necessarily a direct correlation between a profile and some "shoulds" ("I should *always* try to learn by reading, or on my own, or in groups, or at night"). Nor is such precision necessarily a desired outcome. One's preferred environments and ways of learning may need to be modified or compensated for in order to learn successfully in a wide variety of settings and for a wide variety of purposes. What style and its instrumentation do hold out is the promise of help in making choices about how, when, and where to learn (Candy 1980; Dunn and Dunn 1977).

This kind of self-knowledge is also useful for helping other people (e.g., instructors and resource persons) to help one to learn success-fully—one way in which learning style relates to learning how to learn. Adults are increasingly taking the initiative by urging programming agencies and instructors to take learning style into account (Griffin 1979).

Finally, a word is in order concerning teaching style—a less re-searched and clarified sister concept. The term refers to an instructor's characteristic behavior in the teaching-learning situation. There is some evidence that teachers tend to begin an instructional session with the kind of learning activity that they themselves prefer when learning and then generally gravitate toward other methods they find useful. But it cannot be assumed that an individual will always instruct in the same way that he or she learns best. The role demands of one's posi-tion (lecturing is a norm in some institutions) may affect natural incli-nation. Categorizations of instructors that have been proposed include the didactive versus the evocative and the theoretical versus the quali-tative. The complexities involved in separating individual learning style from teaching style may account for the relative paucity of re-search concerning the latter (Brundage 1980; Cross 1976; Kirby 1979). Appendix I lists four teaching-style inventories.

In this chapter I sought to demonstrate that learning style is a viable concept with important implications for both adult educators and learners. The implications include possibilities for achieving better understanding of oneself as learner and for helping others to facilitate one's learning—as Zorba tried to do for his English employer by stat-ing how he (Zorba) learns best. Some theoretical and research bases of the style concept were reviewed. The three major components of style—the cognitive, the affective, and the environmental—were explored. The growing body of style-assessment inventories was introduced, and suggestions were made for using these inventories and the data they yield.

Part II

Developing Learning Skills
and Understandings

In Part I the theoretical bases of the learning how to learn concept were explored. Part II will treat practical applications of learning how to learn—what the individual needs to know and be able to do in order to learn effectively in various modes and settings. The two final chapters, comprising Part III, will deal with helping others learn how to learn—training theory and training exercises.

4

Getting Started

People frequently face decisions about what and where to learn. Consider the latter first. In most communities many options are available—opportunities so broad and diverse that Ronald Gross devoted half of *The Lifelong Learner* to their identification and description, saying that they constitute an invisible university. Many new delivery systems have appeared in recent years. Some are as elaborate as adult degrees packaged in special ways—a baccalaureate in the form of a weekend college, for example. People learn by computer, telephone, radio, audiotapes, and videotapes. About one million people take credit and noncredit courses via television each year. Through Elderhostel, people over sixty participate in one-week (usually summertime) residential courses on a broad range of subjects at 250 colleges in forty states.

An estimated 300,000 people yearly enroll in free universities—informal course programs that have emerged (at least in part) as a response to dissatisfaction with rigidity in higher education. Their motto is Anyone Can Teach, Anyone Can Learn; the subjects explored are almost as wide ranging as life itself.

Learning networks reach many thousands of adults. Also called learning exchanges, these organizations share a common philosophy with free universities but employ a different structure. They are usually a telephone referral service that links potential teachers and learners for instruction on a one-to-one basis (Draves 1980).

Nonetheless, it is impossible to anticipate accurately what adult education opportunities will be available in a particular region or local community. New agencies and programs appear each year, and educational brokering offices are being established to help people to understand the options and locate resources. But many agencies disappear and change their names, their addresses, or their purposes. For this reason we do not attempt here to provide much in the way of specific up-to-date information. Fortunately, three major sources of help are almost always available: public libraries, county cooperative extension offices, and schools and colleges with adult education programs. Librarians can point the way to materials on all subjects, to catalogs of institutions, and to entire books devoted to self-assessment and personal growth processes (for example, Bolles 1978; Gross 1977; Hagberg and Leider 1978; Knowles 1975; Tough 1980). Extension advisers usually have a good grasp of educational opportunities available locally as well as access to the many resources available from state and local governments. Not all adult educators in schools and colleges actively solicit clients for educational counseling, but most are willing to help when asked.

Success in using advisers, counselors, and librarians for better understanding of the options will depend on foresight and persistence. It is wise to use more than one source of information and to locate persons who avoid overselling their own programs. Thinking in advance about one's needs and how to express them increases the chance for success. The telephone can be used to get good information and, of course, to make appointments for counseling. And when meeting with advisers or counselors, it is useful to admit failure to understand something that is said.

Realms to Explore

With many resources available to most people, deciding where to learn may well be easier than deciding what to learn by clarifying interests and desired outcomes. The heading of this section is borrowed from Allen Tough's *Expand Your Life: A Pocket Book for Personal Change* (1980). The phrase seems felicitous when compared with "Deciding What to Learn" or "Clarifying Purposes for Learning." Tough's realms include the following:

Know Thyself: Experiencing Your Mind and Body—activities that provide insight into one's behavior, body states, and feelings (getting in touch with oneself). May involve learning to control anger, tension, or becoming more assertive.

Exploring the Major Fields of Knowledge—the major subject matter fields usually associated with learning in schools and colleges (for example, anthropology, psychology, history, philosophy, literature, international affairs, and economics).

Deepening Personal Relationships—the arts of friendship, intimacy, and love. Includes "parenting."

Learning How to Help Others to a Better Life—learning for increased effectiveness in problem solving, community service, and social action.

Focusing on Religious and Spiritual Growth—learning related to a faith one already embraces, the appreciation of other religions, a search for meaning in life, or transcendent experience.

Getting Enjoyment, Fun, and Happiness Out of Life—learning for self-expression and recreation through such pursuits as dance, gardening, collecting, and painting. Examining these categories and the wide variety of activities that Tough suggests is one way to identify educational interests. Figure 3 presents an instrument (adapted from Hagberg and Leider) for drawing out or pointing toward interests that one may not have been aware of.

The developmental stages and tasks of adulthood mentioned in chapter 2 offer a perspective and directions for clarifying interests and purposes for education. Malcolm Knowles links life's major roles to needed abilities.

Role	*Competencies*
Learner	Reading, writing, computing, perceiving, conceptualizing, evaluating, imagining, inquiring
Becoming a self (with unique self-identity)	Self-analyzing, sensing, goal building, objectivizing, value clarifying, expressing
Friend	Loving, empathizing, listening, collaborating, sharing, helping, giving feedback, supporting
Citizen	Caring, participating, leading, decision making, acting, "conscientizing," discussing, having perspective (historical and cultural)
Family member	Maintaining health, planning, managing, helping, sharing, buying, saving, loving, taking responsibility
Worker	Career planning, technical skills, using supervision, giving supervision, getting along with people, cooperating, planning, delegating, managing
Leisure-time user	Knowing resources, appreciating the arts and humanities, performing, playing, relaxing, reflecting, planning, risking (Knowles 1980b, pp. 266–67)

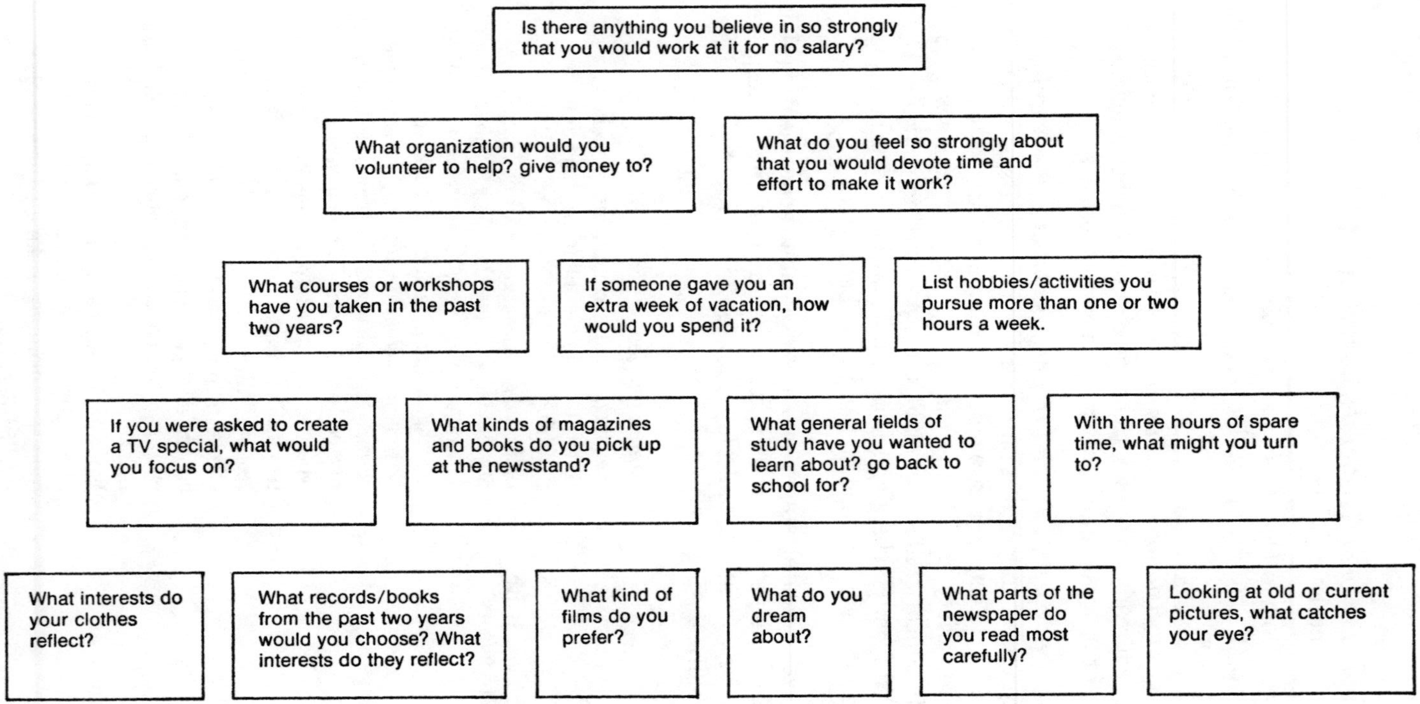

Is there anything you believe in so strongly that you would work at it for no salary?

What do you feel so strongly about that you would devote time and effort to make it work?

What organization would you volunteer to help? give money to?

List hobbies/activities you pursue more than one or two hours a week.

If someone gave you an extra week of vacation, how would you spend it?

With three hours of spare time, what might you turn to?

What courses or workshops have you taken in the past two years?

What kinds of magazines and books do you pick up at the newsstand?

What general fields of study have you wanted to learn about? go back to school for?

Looking at old or current pictures, what catches your eye?

If you were asked to create a TV special, what would you focus on?

What records/books from the past two years would you choose? What interests do they reflect?

What kind of films do you prefer?

What do you dream about?

What parts of the newspaper do you read most carefully?

What interests do your clothes reflect?

Fig. 3. Interests Pyramid

The more concretely one can identify aspirations and assess related levels of competence, the more precisely one can identify what one wants to learn. For this reason, it can be useful to see education and learning in the context of what has come to be called life planning or midcareer planning—a major self-assessment, often undertaken in middle adulthood. Self-assessment involves examining one's own history of work, family and interpersonal relationships, values, interests, and priorities. The individual often receives counseling and takes part in exercises designed to clarify present values and aspirations, blocks to achieving goals, and desirable personal changes for the upcoming period of life. In this larger context, educational needs and interests tend to emerge naturally as means to other desired outcomes. For example, one may come to the decision to put less energy or more energy into his or her vocation—or to change vocations. Each alternative usually points toward an educational need such as learning for a new kind of job or job upgrading, or learning for purposes of self-expression and avocational enjoyment (Bolles 1978; Hagberg and Leider 1978). The steps in the career-change process can look like this:

1. Self-awareness and career awareness developed

2. Plans formulated

3. Education pursued

4. Job search undertaken and placement achieved.

Counseling and other forms of education may well be needed at each step.

Crucial Skills

In addition to acquiring a working knowledge of available educational opportunities and a perspective on personal interests and purposes for learning, becoming a more skillful learner usually involves sharpening skills one already possesses. Some of these—such as discussion skills or skills in answering exam questions—are needed in particular educational settings. But two skills—reading and listening—play a central role in the great share of learning that most people do. To be sure, learning will not be the primary purpose of all reading and listening; but when it is, comprehension and meaningfulness will be strongly affected by reading and listening ability.

Active Listening. Active listening involves hearing words that are spoken and going beyond those words. It requires making an effort to get at the speaker's intended message and paying attention to matters nonverbal as well as verbal.

The kind of listening that facilitates learning is characterized by two seemingly contradictory attributes: it is both empathetic and evaluative. The listener seeks to suspend negative attitudes and preconceptions and enter into dialogue with the speaker—to encourage the speaker to communicate effectively and to grasp what the speaker intends to communicate. At the same time, the active listener weighs what is being said in order to judge its relevance and see how it relates to previous experience and personal learning purposes. The need for combining evaluation and empathy applies in situations as different as listening to an audiotape, attending a lecture, talking with a counselor, or participating in discussion (Apps 1978; Dale 1978).

Active Reading. In much the same way that good listeners interact with speakers and what is said, active readers enter into a transaction with the printed word and employ what they already know in order to learn through reading. They constantly put questions to themselves (What would be an example? Does that relate to any of the stated course objectives?). They are alert to bias and propaganda, noting emotional language and unsubstantiated claims. And they watch for opportunities to apply new ideas as soon as possible.

Skilled readers can shift gears and proceed at differing rates. They scan material in order to glean specific information or identify sections needing further attention. When an instructor holds them responsible for the content of a book, they can read it rapidly the first time and more intensively the second time, or they can implement a comparable strategy of their own that gets results.

Asking four kinds of questions about a piece of writing can help develop more active reading habits and facilitate learning.

- What is this article, chapter, or book about? What is the central theme?
- What are some of the main ideas?
- Is the content believable? What seems unconvincing, faulty, or incomplete?
- Of what value is the piece for my purposes?
- Is it important for my purposes? Why or why not?
  (Adapted from Apps 1978, pp. 57–58)

Appendix B is an exercise for learning to read books more actively.

A third skill should perhaps be included with the skills of listening and reading: observing. One often hears, "I learn a lot by just keeping my eyes open." And one can learn a lot about, say, a neighborhood, a college campus, or nature in general through careful observation. But it is often difficult to really "see." In the following passage, the Indian educator Jiddu Krishnamurti contends that skill in learning requires periodic renewal of the ability to see things freshly along with cultivation of the capacity to suspend the memory of that which was previously learned.

> By listening to what is being said and by watching ourselves a little bit, we learn something, we experience something; and from that learning and experiencing we look. [But] we look with the memory of what we have learned and with what we have experienced; with that memory in mind we look. Therefore it is not looking, it is not learning. Learning implies a mind that learns each time anew. So it is always fresh to learn. Bearing that in mind we are not concerned with the cultivation of memory but rather to observe and see what actually takes place. We will try to be very alert, very attentive, so that what we have seen and what we have learned doesn't become a memory with which we look, and which is already a distortion. Look each time as though it were the first time! (Krishnamurti 1971, p. 121)

Much easier said than done, but a very interesting and instructive challenge.

Cultivating Openness to Change

Knowing our options and possessing some key learning skills will not come to much if we fail to venture forth, if we remain reluctant to expose ourselves to a wide variety of resources and experiences (Tough 1982).

Highlighting people's ambivalence toward growing and changing, the late Abraham Maslow speaks in *Toward a Psychology of Being* of "the need to know and the fear of knowing." He believed that the tendency to avoid personal growth usually stems from fears and feelings of inadequacy that can cause us to deny our best side—to deny our talents, potentialities, creativeness, and finest impulses (Maslow 1968, p. 60). And Carl Rogers terms continuing openness to experience the "most socially useful learning in the modern world" (Rogers 1969, p. 163).

How can we cultivate and revive the curiosity and the experimental attitude toward living and learning that seem to come naturally in childhood? There is obviously no pill that will do the trick. Self-help books and short courses may make contributions. But the kind of attitude that welcomes exposure to new ideas and experience probably cannot be taught. It comes about through a process, the result of an ongoing series of day-to-day decisions—deciding to read that unfamiliar kind of book, to view that film we are not immediately drawn to, to engage in conversation with that person whose beliefs we don't hold, or to visit strange territory. The more we reach out, the easier we find it to reach out again.

> Risk brings its own rewards: the exhilaration of breaking through, of getting to the other side, the relief of a conflict healed, the clarity when a paradox dissolves. . . . Eventually we know deeply that the other side of every fear is a freedom. Finally, we must take charge of the journey, urging ourselves past our own reluctance and misgivings and confusion to new freedom. Once that happens . . . we are on a different life journey. (Ferguson 1980, p. 294)

Choosing the Mode of Learning

Adults need criteria for deciding when to undertake personal learning projects, when to learn collaboratively, or when to enroll in educational institutions. The choice between learning in the self-directed, collaborative, or institutional mode obviously has implications for satisfaction and success in learning.

Self-directed Learning. To conduct a personal learning project is to be both educator and learner at once. One creates knowledge and tests it oneself (Griffin 1979). This mode requires assertiveness and a sense of direction (Knox 1979). The individual attempts to establish optimum conditions for learning and seeks to apply knowledge of personal learning style in ways that make for success.

John Vincent, one of the founders of the chautauqua movement, gave a ringing endorsement for assuming control of one's own learning a hundred years ago.

> I am going to college! Never mind about thirty years, or fifty, or seventy: I am going to college. Harvard? No, nor Yale. . . . [To] my own college, in my own house, taking my own time . . . turning my kitchen, sitting-room, and parlor into college-halls. . . . What a *campus* I have! green fields and forests. . . . What professors I have, in books! . . . My neighbors, the richest of them and the poorest, the most humble and ignorant, and the most scholarly, shall [also] be my pro-

fessors. I will ask questions about everything, and of every-
body, till I find out what I want to know. (Grattan 1959, pp.
70–71)

Michael Rossman waxes lyrical over the prospect of self-directed
learning.

> The learner . . . learns as much by the process of his own
> creation as by recreating others' past learning. . . . His learn-
> ing in a subject takes him deep in its penetration of his self,
> and outward in its embodiment in society. He grows along his
> subject as a vine does along a trellis, over many years and
> windings. (Rossman 1973, p. 28)

However, David Little (1979) cautions that adults must often look to
the most efficient means of learning, making self-education more a
luxury than a reality for most.

In addition to possibly proving inefficient, self-directed learning can
turn out to be difficult and frustrating. For example, to teach oneself a
foreign language is indeed a formidable challenge for almost anyone.
However, the disadvantages inherent in this mode of learning are very
often far outweighed by the convenience, flexibility, absence of institutional requirements, and the sense of satisfaction from achieving one's
purposes while being in control; increasing the ability to carry out
personal learning projects can be richly rewarding. Personal projects
are most appropriate choices when motivation is high and when one
already knows a bit about what is to be learned, at least enough to get
meaningful planning and action under way with dispatch. The availability and cost of alternative modes of learning obviously affect the
decision as well.

Collaborative Learning.   At its best, or when it is reasonably well
carried out, this mode offers opportunities to learn in a mutually supportive climate, one in which one can safely express opinions, test
ideas, try new behavior, and give and get help as needed. It enables the
curiosity, experience, and problem-solving abilities of several people to
be released and harmonized in order to achieve mutual purposes while
meeting individual needs. Interpersonal relationships and communication are of central concern. One learns with and through other people—perhaps as much as from resources outside the group or brought
into the group. While the great share of self-directed learning tends to
be concerned with skills acquisition, collaborative learning tends to
center in activity related to the exploration of ideas and opinions and
to finding solutions to problems. Changes in values, attitudes, and

understandings are often the expected outcome, as opposed to the rapid encompassing of a body of subject matter. Willingness to take risks and the ability to listen actively are called for. And a group may be helpful for clarifying personal interests and reasons for changing or for assessing personal potential.

This mode of learning can also rekindle interest and increase commitment, often providing a change of pace from directing one's own learning or from learning through instruction. The learner has less autonomy than when directing personal learning projects but more than is usually encountered in the institutional setting. However, meeting personal learning needs requires helping others to meet their needs at the same time.

Learning Through Educational Institutions. Schools and colleges were established to serve a youthful clientele. Some have come to tolerate adults; some have decided to welcome them and make accommodations to their interests, life-styles, and characteristics as learners.

To learn through an institution is to enter a world that presupposes considerable external authority, and, in credit programs, tends to involve competition among learners. It is the institution's responsibility to plan programs, establish standards, and employ a variety of administrative practices (e.g., record keeping); it is the learner's responsibility to adjust to the demands and requirements accompanying this mode of learning. As with buying a ready-made coat, a perfect fit does not always occur—in this case the fit is between learners, courses, instructors, and programs. But alterations and adjustments can be made; educational institutions are increasingly making adjustments easier.

A school or college represents a large collection of potential resources for in-depth learning and conferring credentials. The people resources (e.g., faculty) usually have responsibilities that go beyond instruction and the facilitation of learning. They conduct research, for example. They are often required to work with large numbers of students. Material resources may be arranged in systems or made available in ways that make them difficult to understand or use on a part-time basis. To learn most efficiently and effectively in a school or college, adults must come to understand the system and its subsystems. Learning in this mode is especially relevant when one's concerns include getting credentials, having access to expertise, and having the motivational benefits of assignments and deadlines.

Major characteristics of the three learning modes can be summarized as follows:

Learning Mode	Salient Features	When Best Used	Possible Obstacle
Self-directed	Learner autonomy; flexibility	When motivation is strong and the subject matter is not overly difficult	Obtaining appropriate resources; devising useful procedures and getting feedback
Collaborative	Interests and needs met with and through others; adult's experience and knowledge are tapped	When the individual wishes to share ideas and opinions; when problems and issues are to be explored	Inadequate leadership; interpersonal conflict and breakdown in communication
Institutional	Direction by experts; many resources available	When in-depth exploration of subject matter is required; when getting credentials is desired; when externally imposed discipline is needed	Institution may be unaware of adults as learners; dependency may be fostered

Flexibility

A successful learner is equally comfortable when carrying out a personal project, collaborating, or receiving formalized instruction—when "flowing with the rhythms of private time and public time" as Virginia Griffin (1979) puts it. He or she is not unlike a traveler who finds enjoyment and reward in journeying alone, with family or friend, or with a tour guide.

In the next three chapters we will look more closely at ingredients for success in learning on one's own, in groups, and in the classroom.

5

Self-directed Learning: Carrying Out Personal Learning Projects

The adult learner of the future will be highly competent in deciding what to learn and planning and arranging his own learning. He will successfully diagnose and solve almost any problem or difficulty that arises. He will obtain appropriate help competently and quickly, but only when necessary.

Allen Tough
The Adult's Learning Projects

Assuming overall control of a learning effort by conducting a personal learning project is something that almost everyone does from time to time, most of us with regularity. Jindra Kulich (1970) has pointed out the central role of self-education throughout recorded history. Becoming a skillful director of one's own learning requires (1) an understanding of the assumptions underlying this mode of learning, including how it differs from collaborative learning and from learning in schools and colleges; (2) an understanding of the processes involved (e.g., planning processes); and (3) gaining greater facility in implementing those processes. The underlying assumptions were explored in the previous chapter.

One way of looking at a learning project is to see it as a problem-solving process, one in which the following competencies outlined by Malcolm Knowles come into play.

1. The ability to develop and be in touch with curiosities. Perhaps another way of describing this skill would be "the ability to engage in divergent thinking."

2. The ability to formulate questions, based on one's curiosities, that are answerable through inquiry (in contrast to questions that are answerable by authority or faith). . . .

3. The ability to identify the data required to answer the various kinds of questions.

4. The ability to locate the most relevant and reliable sources of the required data. . . .

5. The ability to select and use the most efficient means for collecting the required data from the appropriate sources.

6. The ability to organize, analyze, and evaluate the data so as to get valid answers to questions.

7. The ability to generalize, apply, and communicate the answers to the questions raised. (Knowles, 1973, p. 163)

It was mentioned earlier that carrying out a learning project is not necessarily easy. The following three guidelines can help minimize the difficulties that often arise: keep in mind that almost everyone has completed more successful projects than he or she can readily recall; expect some anxiety and frustration; use a planning and implementation system similar to one of those described below. It is also useful to regard the project itself as a means to learning more about self-directed learning; see it as a means to gain greater understanding of the self as learner and of this way of learning.

Planning

Once the decision has been made to pursue a learning project, further decisions need to be made in three areas—goals and purposes, criteria for evaluation, and learning resources and strategies.

For goals and purposes, a learner should ask himself or herself questions like these: Where do I want to go? Why do I want to learn to do it? learn about it? come to understand it? What degree (or level) of skill or understanding do I seek? What will I consider to be satisfactory achievement?

For criteria for evaluation, questions like these would be appropriate: How will I know when I get there? How will I be able to decide the extent to which my goals and purposes are achieved? By tests? scorecards? expert opinion? my own satisfaction? if the family wants it (e.g., Mexican food) served again? if the boss or a friend suggests we play it (e.g., golf) more than once? if I can converse meaningfully about it and explain it to others?

For learning resources and strategies, these would be appropriate questions: What are the ways and means to get there? Shall I read? write a paper? seek coaching? interview someone? view films? conduct a survey? visit a museum? observe an expert doing it?

Although most planning decisions are tentative, the quality of choices made in these three areas will vitally affect the outcome of a project and the amount of satisfaction a learner gets in carrying it out. To be sure, as the planning phase of a project unfolds, other decisions will need to be made, such as where and when to learn.

One way to organize a basic plan can be seen in figures 4 and 5, two modified examples from actual learning projects.

Learning Project: Norway's Seventeenth of May

Why do people of Norwegian descent in this country so often celebrate the Seventeenth of May? Is it an independence day observance, and, if so, from whom and when? I want to know because I have marked or noted this day for years and don't know why.

Goals and Purposes

1. To explore the historical facts of a Norwegian holiday known as the Seventeenth of May.

2. To enjoy the serendipitous findings concerning Norwegian history that might turn up during the investigation.

Resources and Strategies

1. Read library materials on Norwegian history.

2. Write a brief summary of the historical significance of the celebration.

Evaluation

1. Send the summary to my son, who has expressed interest, and see if he finds it useful.

2. Discuss the serendipitous findings with history buffs, Norwegian relatives, and anyone else who will listen. See if I can converse with a basic amount of knowledge that pleases me and doesn't confuse them.

Fig. 4. Sample Plan

Learning Project: Personal Investing

Goals-Purposes

1. To determine three reliable, readily available sources of information for the small ($5,000–15,000) investor (me).
2. To make a personally satisfactory investment decision for some money now in hand.

Learning Resources

Economics professor at the college
Newspapers and magazines
Friends who invest
Library and borrowed books
Experts

Strategies

1. Locate one expert who I can personally consult in each main category of investment—savings and loan, mutual funds, stocks and bonds, real estate, gold and silver.
2. Develop a list of questions to ask the experts that will provide sufficient information for making a personal investment decision.
3. See what resources are available at home.
4. Go to a college professor for advice as to books and materials that may be of help.
5. Ask friends how they would invest their money.
6. Borrow materials from friends and visit the library for other resources.
7. Telephone experts in the different categories of investment to determine what information they can provide and the extent of their availability.

Evidence of Accomplishment

1. Be able to list in writing three sources of information for a small investor and state why they are considered reliable.
2. Identify one expert in each of the five categories for future consultation.
3. Obtain at least an average return on my investment during the first year (long-range evaluation goal).

Fig. 5. Sample Plan

Learner _____ Mary Jones _____ Learning Project or Topic _____ The Dungeons and Dragons Game

Learning Objectives	Learning Resources and Strategies	Target Date for Completion	Evidence of Accomplishment of Objectives
To understand the general goal of game. How do you win?	Conversation with son who has been playing game for two years.	Week 1	Can answer 90 percent of questions son asks me concerning fundamentals of the game.
To become familiar with playing pieces and vocabulary of the game.	Directions for a kindergarten version of game called Dungeons.	Week 2	Am able to discuss hypothetical situations involved in the game.
To understand the more intricate strategies used by experienced players of the game.	Borrow a copy of the Player's Handbook.	Week 3	Can play for two hours without other players finding me to be a drag.
To be able to build a character with realistic attributes to successfully carry out the mission.	Training session with Dungeon Master and son's friend (session will include two other adults).		
To become a player-character beginning a new mission with four other players and Dungeon Master.	Set up real game situation with all necessary equipment, Dungeon Master, and four players.		

Fig. 6. Sample Learning Contract

Learning Contracts

Sometimes it is useful to base a learning project on more precise planning than these two examples reveal, especially when increased competence is the aim. On such occasions learning contracts provide a means for reconciling individual initiative and commitment with the expectations of others—employers or supervisors, for example. An individual can contract with a supervisor to attain a certain level of competence. Even when their projects are not related to the expectations of others, people sometimes find it useful to contract with themselves in order to clarify their intentions. A completed sample contract is presented in figure 6; a blank one is found in Appendix F.

The learning contract does not differ radically from the two plans presented earlier. However, it places more emphasis on the specification of objectives, target dates, and evaluative criteria to be used. Also, the format used and the name *contract* can combine to reinforce commitment, accountability, and the motivation to follow through on a learning project as intended.

Self-Behavior Modification

This approach focuses on the development, elimination, or strengthening of a personal habit. Examples might be found in such behavior as eating, posture, alcohol consumption, smoking, listening, providing emotional support to others, or physical exercise. The procedure combines practical applications of conditioning with the concerns and operations found in the learning contract (i.e., identifying goals, resources, strategies, and evaluation). It is especially applicable when one has relatively high motivation for change and the specific modification of an ingrained habit can be identified—for example, to be able to remember the names of people as they are introduced to me at social gatherings, or to get at least fifteen minutes of vigorous exercise daily.

The behavior-modification process involves planning for a mental set that will foster change by answering a series of questions, practicing the new or alternative behavior, and rewarding or punishing oneself as needed until the old behavior has been dropped or modified or a new behavior has been acquired. Reinforcement and rewards should come as soon after the desirable behavior as possible. Many small rewards are usually more effective than an occasional big one. These kinds of questions serve as a basis for planning. What skill or behavior do I wish to gain (for example, to stop referring to females as "girls")? Why do I wish to change? What are the advantages of changing? What obstacles will need to be overcome to achieve my objective? Should I announce my intended change to others? Should I ask them to report on my progress? What rewards or punishments will be built into the process? Can day-to-day positive reinforcement be supplied by the use of such procedures as checklists and records of progress? (McLagan 1978, pp. 85–88)

Implementing Plans

As with planning, carrying out a learning project will actually involve many small steps and different activities, among them, communicating, processing information, modifying plans, and improvising. Delineating this process and attempting to provide clues for the successful negotiation of each step is beyond the scope of this book. We spoke earlier in chapter 4 of the importance of listening, reading, observing, and viewing, as actively and flexibly as possible. Successful implementation of a project will also usually require using another person as a resource, getting reliable feedback (to assess progress and adjust procedures), and coping with blocks and obstacles that may emerge along the way.

Using Another Person as a Resource for Learning.   The resource person may be a professional (physician, librarian, broker, teacher, mechanic) or a gifted amateur (stamp collector, traveler, seamstress, cook, Civil War buff). He or she may have volunteered to help, been hired to help, or consented to fit a little time for helping into a busy schedule. The interactions may vary from brief telephone conversations to a sustained series of interviews or tutorial sessions.

The ideal person should be one from whom a learner could smoothly obtain the greatest amount of assistance related to the purposes and goals of the project. Such a person should be easy to establish a rapport with and to communicate with. The help provided should be appropriate for the learner's present level of knowledge and skill. The learner's efforts should be encouraged, his or her doubts should be allayed, and useful feedback concerning progress should be readily available. A learner may have to use ingenuity in seeking out and getting what is feasible and fair to ask of those who agree to help.

In considering people as possible resources, a skilled learner asks questions like, Does the person apparently have the necessary knowledge or skill to be helpful? Can I communicate to him or her what I wish to know or to be able to do? Can I expect to be reasonably comfortable with this person and he or she with me?

When preparing for an encounter with a resource person, the potential for optimum learning can be enhanced by clarifying as precisely as possible the help that is sought and by trying to foresee potential problems in communicating clearly and efficiently—for example, lack of technical vocabulary (will presenting the resource person with a written list of questions help or hinder?). The potential for optimum learning can also be enhanced by considering what learning environment—the office, the home, a particular location in the home—and time of day are preferred.

When interacting with a resource person, it is important for the learner to make his or her needs as clear as possible and to make it known when the resource person is on target. A skilled learner is moderately assertive: "That's very helpful." "I'm afraid I don't understand." "Could you repeat that last point?" "What would be an example of that?" "May I try to summarize?" "May I try it now?" "I learn well from diagrams." "Am I asking the right questions?" "What do you think I ought to do next?"

It is useful for a learner to put himself or herself in the resource person's place. Unless the resource person is providing a paid service, the rewards in the transaction (and the willingness to continue to put effort into it) will derive from such factors as knowing that the help is really helpful, seeing that progress is made by the learner, and feeling that one is not being inappropriately used. A learner's rewards are likely to be dependent on the extent to which the resource person also meets with rewards; and a learner can control only what he himself does.

When a relationship is not panning out, what's to be done? Suppose the knowledge is not there, the resource person cannot (or is too busy to) teach what he or she knows, or the chemistry is not right. The learner must disengage with dispatch and with tact. He or she can look elsewhere and also consider what has been learned about the process of learning from a resource person (perhaps learning that one shouldn't try to learn from a family member or from a friend who doesn't take one seriously). Fortunately, research shows that people tend to become even more persistent in seeking help after experiencing setbacks (Tough 1979).

Getting Feedback.   Finding out how one is getting on with the learning project is obviously important because it is directly related to motivation, satisfaction, and achievement. In a class or a discussion group, feedback is usually available from an authority or from peers. When it is not forthcoming, a learner can request it. But obtaining relevant information can present a problem when conducting a personal project.

If a plan includes clear goals, target dates, and relatively specific criteria for evaluation, the groundwork has been laid for getting reliable and realistic feedback as a project unfolds. This is especially true when the purpose is to learn a skill or change a habit. With a typing project (that calls, for example, for learning to type after three months at a rate of thirty words per minute with a maximum of one error) a learner can either self-test or show a sample to someone. Plans that call for the use of programmed materials (e.g., a book with built-in tests and answers or a computerized module) or videotaping an activity and playing it back make the obtaining of feedback a relatively easy matter. Projects directed toward less tangible outcomes (appreciating Stravinsky, understanding the cold war, becoming more assertive) require extra effort in the planning phase to build in the kinds of goals and criteria that make feasible the assessment of progress.

When the purpose of a project is merely to explore a subject—to see what's there—making specific plans to obtain feedback is not always feasible or desirable. Often a personal sense of satisfaction will suffice. At other times failure to obtain useful feedback may become a central concern. To the extent that planning for the provision for feedback has not occurred, improvisation will be necessary. A learner then needs to be alert for clues as to how well he or she is doing and what adjustments in plans or strategies need to be made. He or she may need to let a helper know that more frequent or precise feedback is desired. A learner may need to stop and ask, "If I'm not sure how well I'm progressing, what might help me find out? Since this resource person tends to provide less feedback than I need, how can I work around the problem? By taking steps to get it from him or her? By getting it elsewhere?"

Concerning the specifying of the feedback desired, a personal example comes to mind. I asked a friend for a reaction to a draft of the first chapter of this book but provided no guidelines. The resulting comments were not very helpful. When asking for a reaction to chapter 2, I requested an evaluation of the accuracy of the information presented, suggestions for additions or deletions, and the identification of passages that were particularly difficult to understand. This time the feedback proved to be quite useful and more cheerfully forthcoming.

When a learner assesses his or her own progress, the signs that learning has transpired include the following: the learner can state something in his or her own words, can ask meaningful questions concerning the subject (having more questions than one began with can be a sign of progress), can state with some precision what he or she still does not know or cannot do, and wants to share what has been learned with others.

Sometimes, especially when learning a skill, it is useful to construct an instrument for self-rating or for rating by others. Repeating the learning task (giving a speech, for example) and then applying the rating tool will provide continuing feedback as to progress and areas still needing improvement. And the building of the rating tool may well turn out to be a helpful learning project within a learning project. Malcolm Knowles provides some helpful guidelines and sample instruments in his book *Self-Directed Learning.*

Coping with Blocks and Obstacles.   Some blocks or unexpected obstacles usually emerge as a project unfolds, especially when it is of considerable duration and complexity. Directions may prove hard to follow, a learner may have difficulty obtaining or using a piece of equipment or may lack a quiet place to read, a resource may prove unsatisfactory, an instrumental task too difficult, or a concept abstruse, support from family members may fail to materialize. It is usually necessary to improvise strategies for coping with matters of this kind.

One problem that learners frequently report is finding more printed or audiovisual materials available on a topic than they know what to do with. Materials may also be overly technical or too detailed. However, learning project goals and purposes can provide a basis for making selections. The ability to scan will be helpful. One strategy is to find an introductory book designed for children in order to get an overview of the concepts, terms, and parameters of a subject. The person who is not embarrassed to use the children's room of a public library has an advantage in exploring new areas of knowledge.

A very common problem in self-directed learning is wavering motivation. The absence of a major goal (e.g., to get a degree or a certificate) and of the external direction and reinforcement that good instruction or a compatible group of peers can provide can be keenly felt. Initial enthusiasm may erode rapidly if a project proves unexpectedly difficult or if other commitments require that it be set aside.

Knowledgeable learners expect cycles in motivation and plateaus in achievement. They monitor their learning behavior for clues as to patterns, tendencies, and potential pitfalls. They develop strategies for rekindling interest and commitment—varying the learning tasks, changing the pace or location for learning, assessing how far they've come as well as how far they have to go, granting themselves rewards. They may decide to seek diagnostic help or to modify their plan (to join a group, form a group, or enroll in a course, for example). They may review personal learning style in relation to resources and strategies that have been employed thus far. They may ask a friend how he or she copes with a temporary loss of motivation. And they aren't

Post Project Analysis Form

Project _____ Date Completed _____

Activity	Need for Improvement Next Time		
	Little	Some	Much
1. Determining what to learn	_____	_____	_____
2. Clarifying goals and purposes	_____	_____	_____
3. Specifying evaluative criteria	_____	_____	_____
4. Identifying resources	_____	_____	_____
5. Appraising the usefulness of resources	_____	_____	_____
6. Deciding when to seek help	_____	_____	_____
7. Choosing strategies	_____	_____	_____
8. Execution of strategies			
a. Interviewing and questioning	_____	_____	_____
b. Reading	_____	_____	_____
c. Listening	_____	_____	_____
d. Observing	_____	_____	_____
e. Viewing	_____	_____	_____
f. Practicing a skill	_____	_____	_____
g. Obtaining feedback	_____	_____	_____
h. Devising ways around blocks	_____	_____	_____
i. Creating a suitable learning environment	_____	_____	_____
j. Applying what I learn	_____	_____	_____
k. Other _____	_____	_____	_____

9. Did the decision to carry out a personal learning project prove to be a sound one? Would group or classroom learning have been a better choice?

10. What are one or two key insights I've gained about this kind of learning?

Fig. 7. Checklist for Self-administered Training

unduly hard on themselves if a project doesn't work out, seeking to learn what might make the next one more effective and pleasurable.

Evaluating for Increased Learning Skill

The chances of a learning project's contribution to skill in self-directed learning itself will increase if opportunities for this to happen are built in. Time can be set aside at the end of each learning episode and at the project's end to look at the process (how one went about it) as well as the content (what was learned). It is useful to reflect on what might be done differently the next time. Figure 7 provides a basis for such analysis.

Successful direction of one's own education and learning requires skill in carrying out learning projects—the ability to plan, conduct, and evaluate. Ways to try to ensure systematic planning and follow-through include the use of learning contracts and self-behavior modification. It is useful to know how to use another person as a resource for learning and how to obtain reliable feedback concerning progress.

6

Learning Collaboratively

Probably no greater need exists than to learn how to participate effectively. Many studies have shown that humans are, and always have been, social animals.

James W. Botkin
No Limits to Learning

A frequently used figure of speech to describe the effective learning group is a "learning team." The members work well together, seek to compensate for one another's shortcomings, utilize the contributions of all to achieve common goals, and try to improve performance as they go along. Achieving learning goals and accomplishing learning-related tasks depend on such matters as coordination (or leadership), communication, appropriateness of resources and procedures, and resolving together of the conflicts that almost inevitably arise. Somewhere along the way, the members must establish a degree of mutual trust.

Optimum Conditions

A learning group differs from a task group (for example, a board of review or an infantry platoon) by virtue of the relatively greater importance of meeting individual needs for change and growth en route to common goals and purposes. The group is not primarily concerned with achieving the purposes of one individual or of a larger organization. Individuals tend to realize the most personal benefit from learning in groups to the extent that the following four conditions are present.

106

1. *Everyone shares in the program development and evaluation.* All members accept responsibility for identifying what is to be learned, why it is to be learned (goals), how it is to be learned (resources and procedures), and for the evaluative criteria employed. Designated or temporarily empowered leaders do a minimum of planning for other members and a maximum of planning with them. Leadership tends to be either shared (group centered) or rotated.

2. *Freedom of expression is allowed.* A climate exists in which learners can disagree, ask for help, and try out new ideas and behavior. People are not volunteered for responsibilities. There is little need to be defensive. One can express feelings that relate to facilitating change and achieving group purposes. And the members seldom abuse this freedom, knowing that responsibility goes with liberty.

3. *Group members possess the skills of joint inquiry and problem-solving.* They talk and they also listen actively. They hear one another. They know how to lead discussion, reach consensus, and use one another as resources for learning. They know how to ask for, give, and receive feedback.

4. *A diagnostic attitude toward processes is encouraged.* The group members attend to group functions and problems—how the group is doing as well as what is being done and learned. Opportunities are provided for analysis of progress and possible changes in goals or procedures. People are encouraged to apply their learning, to develop process skills, to examine their experiences in the group, and to get training for member roles as needed.

When people share in program development, they acquire a stake in an educational venture (a discussion is shared, a goal becomes something each learner wishes to help achieve because he or she helped to set it). Freedom of expression is a necessary condition for the sharing process to take place. The skills of joint inquiry enable learners to participate meaningfully in planning and evaluative processes and to learn from the resources and procedures used to explore ideas and problems. If a diagnostic attitude toward all of these matters is maintained, the chances are best of achieving group goals while meeting personal needs.

Let's look at an example of the failure to activate these optimum conditions for collaborative learning.

A Case Study

The pastor of his church suggests that Bill Williams consider forming and leading a young couples group in which everyday problems in living will be discussed in relation to the teachings of the church. Bill has been tapped because he is energetic, pleasant, willing to serve, and knows his Bible. He accepts the challenge and enlists eight couples for a series of weekly meetings.

Bill makes almost all the key decisions—about what topics are to be explored, for example. He selects printed materials for each session from the church library. He leads each session, calling on people, often evaluating their answers, and suggesting where the Scriptures will help them. There is little interaction among the members, who begin to show less and less enthusiasm at each succeeding session. One or two suggest alternative ways of proceeding but receive little encouragement. The one person who ventures into the expression of feelings meets with resistance and rejection.

When members (did they ever really belong?) begin dropping out, Bill finally experiments. He asks a group member to lead the next session, at which he himself refrains from speaking, sensing that he has been too dominant thus far. The results are even more disastrous as confused group members alternate between halting discussion and puzzled looks at the leader they've become dependent on. When one member suggests that they analyze the situation, no one supports her. After one more session the group dissolves amid apathy, frustration, and guilt.

In this example, those participating clearly lacked the opportunity and the skills to share in program development. A climate of freedom and mutual support was never established, despite the fact that Bill was a nonthreatening nice guy. And advocacy for the adoption of a diagnostic attitude came too late.

When a person who has learned how to learn collaboratively provides leadership in the formation of a learning group, he or she can help ensure that efforts are made to activate the optimum conditions for this mode of learning. It may also be feasible to bring in consultative assistance to establish or reinforce these guidelines. However, in most instances experience with collaborative learning comes about by entering an already existing group. When one encounters a group in which the conditions for learning are far from ideal, two courses of action, in addition to dropping out, will present themselves: one can either seek to effect changes or undertake to learn as much as possible despite the situation. The options are not mutually exclusive. To initiate change (facilitate collaborative learning), the learner can do the following:

1. Ask diagnostic questions when opportunities present themselves ("Has there been a problem finding suitable resources before?" "Can we review the goals?" "What is our usual procedure for evaluating?").

2. Model the behavior of the person skilled in collaborative learning (e.g., summarizing, initiating requests for personal feedback, supporting others, building on others' comments, listening actively).

3. Suggest that one or more sessions be given over to taking stock of the group's progress and possible needs for adjustment in goals or procedures.

4. Should a leadership role be offered, make it a condition for acceptance that the group increase its concern for the process of learning.

To learn as much as possible despite unfavorable conditions, it is helpful to do the following:

1. Keep one's own purposes and goals clearly in mind, extracting from each session what contributes most to their attainment.

2. Cultivate a certain amount of detachment, using the group learning experience as a resource for acquiring content and as a kind of laboratory for sharpening diagnostic skills related to learning processes. (The learner could ask himself or herself: "What is the effect of the dependence on Robert's Rules of Order?" "What alternate structure would help?" "Why is consensus so difficult to achieve?" "Where does the real leadership come from?")

Serving as a Leader

Leadership is activity contributing to goal attainment. Some leadership in collaborative learning should—and usually does—come from everyone who participates. But designated leader roles—chair, coordinator, leader—are commonly utilized. The effective leader keeps in mind that his or her tasks are to help people learn; to tap the experience and knowledge present in the group; to help create an environment for learning; to facilitate decision making in ways that reconcile group progress with individual needs (for example, needs for recognition, acceptance, and a sense of usefulness); and to help the group members help one another to clarify goals, find resources, and utilize procedures that will foster change and growth.

One's skills for these tasks do not remain constant—something achievable and forever available when one is in the leader role. Rather, what is involved are understandings, attitudes, and skills requiring continual improvement, or renewal, and flexible application at different times in different groups. It may also be useful to seek or devise training opportunities as needed.

Discussion Leadership. All groups offer opportunities for talk; considerable effort usually goes into conducting business and into decision making about plans and procedures. By *discussion* here, however, we refer to the collaborative effort to explore a topic or problem for purposes of learning.

Preparation to lead a discussion can be facilitated by asking such questions as, Do the room arrangement and seating lend themselves to direct interaction and conversation by the members (face-to-face seating is necessary; a chalkboard usually helps)? Are the members well enough acquainted to help each other learn? Should a get-acquainted exercise be used?

It is also helpful for the leader to prepare brief introductory remarks aimed at clarifying purposes and goals, stimulating interest, and encouraging active participation. Do the members understand their roles and their responsibilities?

When discussion gets under way, the leader should phrase questions so they cannot be answered by yes or no. Why and how questions tend to bring out discussion better than what, when, or where questions. The leader should avoid answering members' questions unless absolutely necessary (usually referring them back to the group). Occasionally the leader should make a brief summary. He or she should seek to ascertain if people are getting what they want from the discussion, making such adjustments in procedure as consensus permits, and seek to keep conversation relevant to the topic and goals. The leader should consider using the chalkboard to list emerging ideas, areas of agreement or disagreement, and questions for futher inquiry; and he or she should watch for opportunities to facilitate communication and understanding, trying to give everyone a sense of both participation and accomplishment.

Responsible Participation

Collaborative learning requires more than skilled leadership. Each person in the boat pulls an oar. The responsible group member takes the kinds of actions outlined in figure 8.

Communication

- Listens actively
- Helps others understand what is said
- Keeps remarks related to the task at hand

Climate

- Helps to arrange for appropriate physical environment
- Demonstrates support of others
- Expresses feelings in constructive ways
- Lets people be themselves

Openness

- Reveals what he or she wants to learn
- Tries out new ideas and ways of doing things
- Requests personal feedback

Other Behavior

- Shares in program development and evaluation
- Volunteers for special tasks or roles
- Taps the knowledge and experience present in the group and outside resources used
- Shares the responsibility when things go less than well
- Diagnoses learning processes and seeks opportunities to improve process skills

Fig. 8.   Some Behaviors of the Skilled Participant in Collaborative Learning

When they lack access to a learning group that serves their purposes, people can form one. It is common to start one concerning subjects that do not yet exist as a field, perhaps something highly specialized. Ronald Gross in his book *The Lifelong Learner* describes forming a group pertaining to his own interest and vocation—public-interest writing—and sets forth guidelines for so doing (Gross 1977, pp. 109–10).

Planning Processes

Just as with directing one's own learning, the planning of collaborative learning activities—of group discussions, workshops, and conferences, for example—represents an excellent opportunity for learning. It is shortsighted to hurry through planning in order to get to the learning not only because haste makes waste, but because planning is learning. Planners are clarifying their thoughts about a problem, subject, or topic at hand. They often find themselves defining concepts and terms. They evaluate resources for potential usefulness. They come to see new relationships. They examine assumptions and recognize gaps in present knowledge. The need to know becomes reinforced along with readiness to encourage others to participate. The planners' active participation (in "our" program) when the activity is conducted later becomes almost automatically assured. Devoting up to 40 percent of total learning time to planning activity should not be considered unusual or undesirable as long as the planners are reasonably satisfied with their progress.

Collaborative learning activities are best planned either by the total group itself or by a committee representative of those expected to participate. Examples of the latter course might be a group of health professionals planning a workshop for themselves and their colleagues or a committee designing an orientation course for volunteers in a service agency.

Groups that meet in homes or comparable sites can readily involve the total membership in program development. Committees representing larger groups of potential participants often have to discipline themselves to avoid losing sight of the fact that they should plan with and not for other persons. In either instance, following an organized planning system or model can help to bring into being the conditions and activities through which people can profit the most from learning together.

Six Planning Steps. The following system has been tested with hundreds of groups. It is oriented toward planning carried out by a committee representing a larger constituency expected to participate in the activities under design.

Step 1. *Identify a common interest or need of those who will participate.* An interest is something the participants would presumably like to learn about or ought to come to understand better. It may present itself in the form of a problem. Among the most commonly used means of identifying needs and interests are surveys and interviews. The evaluation of a previous educational event often yields clues as well.

Example. A committee of teachers and parents designing a

workshop to be held at their school decided on "Achieving Better Cooperation Between the School and Home."

Step 2. *Develop topics.* Topics are the specific questions, issues, ideas, skills, and concerns with which the learning activity will be involved. Topics are developed by breaking down an interest or a need—usually into questions the group seeks to answer. This constitutes the potential content of the activities or meetings being planned. Stating them as questions almost always proves helpful.

Examples. What are some recurring obstacles to home-school cooperation? What areas readily lend themselves to improved cooperation? How do parents see the role of school personnel? How do school staff members see the parents' role? What kind of initiatives might be taken?

Step 3. *Set goals for the learning activity.* The planners set goals in order to clarify what they hope to accomplish. Goals are the objectives or ends toward which the learning activities are directed. Beginning them with an infinitive (for example, to develop, to stimulate) is usually helpful. So is a degree of specificity. At this point provision for evaluaton is often begun.

Examples. To stimulate awareness and to encourage realistic thinking about home-school relationships. To develop at least three recommendations or action steps that stand to improve our home-school relationships.

Step 4. *Select appropriate resources.* Resources are people and materials from which the learners can seek information. In addition to people, there are films, filmstrips, slides, pictures, exhibits, case histories, annotated reading lists, information briefs, charts, maps, books, pamphlets, and so forth.

Examples. School faculty, administration, and staff. Parents and other community people. Articles or audiovisual aids on home-school cooperation. University faculty member specializing in home-school cooperation.

Step 5. *Select appropriate procedures or strategies.* Procedures or strategies are ways of arranging the relationships of learners and resources to enable people to acquire knowledge in a learning situation. In addition to the information that has emerged from steps 1 through 4 in the planning process, choices now are based on such

Step 1. Interest or Need	Step 2. Topics	Step 3. Goals	Step 4. Resources	Step 5. Procedures or Strategies
Consensus Decision Making	*Topics Generated* What is consensus? How do you recognize valid or nonvalid consensus? What are the ways to check for consensus (silence, ask each person, ask entire group)? Who is most responsible for it? When should consensus be used? When should consensus not be used? What are the conditions for valid consensus? What are the problems in getting consensus? How is it best related to leadership style? What is the effect of time on consensus? *Topics Selected and Ordered for Program Content* What is valid consensus? Under what conditions should it be used (size of group, type of decision, type of leadership, other factors)? What are the conditions for achieving and recognizing consensus issues and problems?	To increase the understanding of the conditions for valid consensus, the problems of achieving it, and when to seek it.	*Persons* Participants' experience *Printed Materials* Sections in a few books	*First Alternative* Speech on "What Is Consensus?" (10 min.) Work groups to identify conditions for achieving consensus (20 min.) Reports from work groups (10 min.) Open forum (10 min.) Evaluation data (5 min.) *Second Alternative* Work groups to identify consensus issues (10 min.) Panel of participants from work groups present and analyze issues (20 min.) Open forum (15 min.) Summary (5 min.) Evaluation data (5 min.)

Step 6. Format and Time Schedule

8:00 Introduction (Jack Jones)
     Program goals
     Procedure to be used
     Forming groups and assigning tasks

8:10 Work groups (four persons each)
     Identify consensus issues

8:20 Panel (Jane Doe, Moderator)
     Present and analyze consensus issues
     Audience participation after 20 min.

8:50 Summary of issues and answers (Jack Jones)

8:55 Evaluation form distributed (Fred Smith)

9:00 Adjournment (Jack Jones)

Fig. 9. Example of the Use of the Six Planning Steps

factors as the anticipated size of the group, the characteristics of those who will participate (including their learning styles), and the available physical facilities. Appendix H is an overview of some procedures, strategies, and desired outcomes for collaborative learning.
Examples. Small groups, role play, the lecture, the panel, the interview, the field trip, demonstration, and viewing films.

Step 6. *Put the main activities into a format and time schedule.* Decisions are made about who is to be responsible for such special tasks as promotion, evaluation, obtaining reading materials, physical arrangements, introducing a speaker, moderating a panel, or leading discussion. (Bergevin, Morris, and Smith 1963)

Figure 9 is an example of a short session planned following this model. It should be noted that the example brings out the need for flexibility in moving through the process, especially at steps 2, 3, and 5. Step 3 is positioned to show the interaction that often transpires between development of topics and the setting of goals.

Evaluation. The six planning steps do not identify evaluation as a separate step because the focus is on planning activities and planning for evaluation can begin at any time. If evaluation is to be done in terms of the extent to which goals are achieved, sometime during or soon after step 3 is the place to begin. However, many groups do not use a goals-attainment approach for evaluation. They may take a less rigorous approach, perhaps relying on participant reaction and observations by committee members. Looking for unintended outcomes can also be useful.

Problems. As the six planning steps are worked through, it is helpful to get feedback concerning how the planners feel about the process, the problems they are encountering, and the adjustments that might be made to make the planning effort more task effective and rewarding. The most common difficulties encountered are briefly summarized in figure 10.

Should the six planning steps prove to be too formal, too cumbersome, or otherwise inappropriate, there are many other planning models in the literature of adult education (for example, see Davis and McCallon 1975; Knowles 1980; Loughary and Hopson 1979; and Mc-

Difficulty	Remedy
Interest or Need Identification	
Planning for, instead of with, other people.	Beginning where people are.
Premature agreement on the interest or need to be addressed.	Careful analysis and effort to get input from potential participants.
Topics Development	
Seeking answers that will come later, when the learning activities are conducted.	Disciplined discussion and sensitive leadership.
Excessive attention to precise wording of topics.	Seeking a middle way. Using question form and sketching out topics provisionally.
Goal Setting	
Goals too vague.	A certain amount of specificity.
Can't tell a goal from a topic.	Beginning each goal statement with an infinitive and phrasing topics as questions.
Resources	
Premature closure with easiest to locate resources selected.	Assessing resources in terms of topics, goals, and learners' characteristics.
Group members neglected as resources.	Finding out what knowledge and experience are present in the planning group and the expected participants.
Procedures-Strategies	
Overreliance on favorites (e.g., the lecture).	Choosing in terms of inherent characteristics of each as they relate to goals, topics, and available resources (see Appendix H).
No procedure seems to fit for a particular purpose.	Modifying or inventing a procedure for a particular purpose.
Format-Outline	
Committee responsibilities not spelled out—who's to do what and when.	Writing responsibilities down.
Inflexible or unrealistic schedule.	Providing alternatives and building in margins.
Failure to let participants know what to expect and what's expected of them.	Spelling out what is expected of participants (in brochures, printed programs, introductions, and instructions).

Fig. 10. Most Common Difficulties with the Use of the Six Planning Steps

Lagan 1978). Regardless of how the matter is approached, it is well to keep three things in mind: planning represents an opportunity to learn; collaborative learning calls for the maximum involvement of learners in program development; and sound design requires thinking about what is to be learned and why (goals) before deciding how (resources and procedures). No resource or strategy is intrinsically valuable for all learning situations. A certain book or a film may rightfully be regarded as a classic and yet be worthless as a resource for learning by a particular group for its particular purposes. Role playing, game playing, and discussion, for example, are not good procedures per se; they are only good for appropriate purposes.

Planners who precede the identification of interests, needs, and goals with the selection of resources and strategies will usually encounter apathy if not resistance to their offerings; and they will be programming those who participate for unnecessary difficulties.

When Groups Need Assistance

In addition to training themselves—through reading, emphasizing process as well as content, and regular diagnostic activity—groups can get training assistance from a variety of sources. Many local churches have skilled staff members, and almost all have expertise in district (synodical) and national offices. YMCAs and YWCAs often have persons knowledgeable about collaborative learning. In colleges and universities, help is most likely to be available from faculty members and advanced graduate students in the fields of communication, group work, adult education, social psychology, human-resource development, organizational development, and extension; they may be found in academic departments and in community-oriented service arms such as the University of Michigan's Survey Research Institute or Indiana University's Bureau of Studies in Adult Education. And private consultants are available in many communities.

To identify and set the priorities where training may be needed, the checklist in figure 11 can be used. The results can be discussed and serve as a basis for action.

The person skilled in collaborative learning knows how to share in program development and possesses a diagnostic attitude toward group processes. He or she can lead and participate responsibly in group discussion and problem-solving activities and knows how to plan learning activities that meet members' needs and interests while achieving group goals.

Training Needs Analysis Form

Here are some matters in which our group may need improvement in order to learn more effectively and enjoyably. What's your reaction?

Area	Need for Improvement		
	Little	Some	Much

General

1. Setting a climate for learning   ____   ____   ____

2. Helping one another learn   ____   ____   ____

3. Tapping members' own knowledge and experience   ____   ____   ____

4. Reaching consensus   ____   ____   ____

Planning, Conducting, and Evaluating

1. Deciding what to learn   ____   ____   ____

2. Clarifying goals and purposes   ____   ____   ____

3. Accessing suitable resources   ____   ____   ____

4. Selecting and employing appropriate strategies and procedures   ____   ____   ____

5. Providing for feedback and evaluation

    a. Getting good information for evaluation   ____   ____   ____

    b. Interpreting the information obtained   ____   ____   ____

    c. Using results of evaluation for further planning   ____   ____   ____

    d. Helping members apply what's learned   ____   ____   ____

Remarks and Suggestions: _____

_____

_____

_____

Fig. 11. Identifying Training Needs for Collaborative Learning

7

Learning Through
Educational Institutions

---

*A quiet revolution is taking place on college and university
campuses across this country. . . . What I'm referring to is
the return of thousands of adults to college campuses,
adults who may have attended college for one or more years
and dropped out, adults who may have received a
baccalaureate degree but find need for additional education,
and adults who may never have attended college.*

Jerold W. Apps
The Adult Learner on Campus

Successfully utilizing schools and colleges for learning requires knowledge of available programs and the ability to evaluate the potential
usefulness of an institution's educational offerings. Once enrolled in a
course or in a certificate or degree program, skilled learners try to tap
its full potential as a resource for learning. This may require sharpening such skills as studying, note-taking, expository writing, and taking
exams. Knowing how to get the most from an instructor and knowing
an adult learner's rights as a student can also be helpful.

Students' Rights

Becoming a consumer of education should entitle an adult to certain
guarantees and prerogatives. At the very least the instruction provided
should be in line with the content described and the purposes set forth
in a brochure, catalog, or course description. When it is not, accountability is in order. And, of course, programs exist to serve those who

enroll, not to meet the needs of instructors or to further the convenience of administrators.

People are not out of line when they ask to talk to instructors about what will take place in a course or ask to see a course outline. They are entitled to query administrators of vocational programs for evidence of the job placement of previous graduates, and they are wise to inquire about services and resources available to regular full-time students that part-time students have access to also (e.g., counseling, learning centers, bookstores, recreation facilities, special events).

The consumer of adult education services may even have occasion to request a full or partial refund—just as he or she has probably done in a store or at a garage. Responsible administrators do not find such requests annoying if they are plausible and made with a modicum of pleasantness. More often than not there proves to be sufficient cause to comply, often for reasons of good public relations.

In assessing the potential usefulness of a course described in a brochure, a learner can do the following:

1. Look for claims that sound excessive in relation to the amount of instructional time allotted. (Learn conversational French in sixteen hours?)

2. Look for specific information about the objectives and about the activities that will be used to help achieve them. (Is a skill supposed to be learned without practice opportunities?)

3. See if the qualifications of the instructor are made clear. (Is there reason to believe that the instructor has experience in teaching adults?)

4. Look for signs that provision will be made for feedback and evaluation.

Once enrolled in a course, students would seem to be entitled to the following:

1. A clear statement of what they are expected to know or be able to do upon completing the course

2. Information about the kind of preparation expected for class sessions as opposed to what the instructor can be expected to provide

3. Opportunities to receive accurate feedback

4. The right to express values and points of view toward subject matter that differ from those of authorities.

Student responsibilities accompanying these rights lie in defining personal goals, preparing for class, taking assignments seriously, meeting minimum objectives, and perhaps letting the instructor know about personal learning style.

Choices and Commitments

When people consider making a commitment to a degree or certificate program, they usually need to search carefully for pertinent information. They may be able to talk to persons already enrolled and to program counselors or administrators. They may even take one or two courses to confirm interest and test for compatibility. And they can try to identify programs that cater to adults.

Many colleges and universities offer degrees or certificates designed for adult audiences. These are sometimes called nontraditional or new-degree programs. Such a program may involve a special curriculum parallel to the one for regular full-time students. Or an existing curriculum may be specially packaged—into telelessons, weekend sessions, or learning modules in learning labs, for example. Alternate ways of earning credit often come into play; one way is called credit for prior learning.

The best of the special programs for adults have five characteristics:

1. Faculty members who are comfortable working with older students, have a sense of mission to make the program work, and have themselves continued to learn.

2. A comprehensive set of support services which may include orientation activities, counseling, financial assistance, how-to-study help, and child-care facilities.

3. Flexible scheduling and curricular options.

4. An adult environment: there are locations for getting together on an informal basis, there is a minimum of red tape (no registration forms that ask for parents' name and address), and the campus bookstore stays open on evenings and weekends.

5. Career assessment and job placement assistance.

When the learners' needs are more modest than obtaining a degree—increased speed in reading or an introduction to classical guitar, for example—they usually search for courses in the adult education program of a secondary school, college, recreation agency, or proprietary (commercial) school. The latter should not be overlooked as a possibility despite the great unevenness of the quality and value of its offerings. In many communities the same subject may be offered by a variety of agencies for a variety of fees. An offering may carry degree-related credit or a kind of credit that is not of much use should a learner later seek to apply it toward a degree, or no credit (sometimes called credit free). Typing or speed-reading may cost two dollars per instructional hour at the high school, four dollars per instructional hour at a community college, and eight to ten dollars per instructional hour at a proprietary school. An appropriate choice will usually be based on such factors as convenience, personal goals and purposes, financial resources, and the reputation of the provider.

Getting the Most from Instruction

It was explained in chapter 5 that successful use of resource people requires empathy, active listening, communicating needs, and letting the resource people know when help is helpful. In the classroom, the resource person becomes an acknowledged expert or a distinguished scholar, but most of the same guidelines apply. Sophisticated students regard instructors as resources and learn to use their instructors' knowledge.

In his article "How to Use a Teacher" in *Pleasures in Learning,* Milton Stern, Dean of Extension at the University of California, offers some suggestions to mature students:

> [Learn to] . . . recognize a difference between introductory and advanced classes. Generally, in basic subject matter, where you as student know very little, often even of the vocabulary of the subject, you would do well to be a blotter, absorbing information and skills. By and large, suspend for a while the use of your critical abilities.
>
> As for classes in which skills are to be learned—they simply are not painless. Drudgery is involved—a pleasant tedium of learning, if you are willing to accept the discipline in the interest of ultimate power, but impossible otherwise.
>
> In an advanced course, on the other hand, an "I'm from Missouri" approach may be more helpful. Scepticism, questioning—all presuming a basis of knowledge on the student's part—such is the attitude to be cultivated.
>
> Beyond such points growing out of subject matter lies the issue of the teacher's personality as expressed in the classroom. Is he a lecturer primarily—overwhelming you, you complain, with facts and more facts? Before you criticize,

make sure that giving the facts isn't the most important job for him to do. It may be that he is not a pedant but that you—with all respect—are undisciplined. Does he go too fast? Or could it be that you haven't done your homework?

Certainly a teacher should be "interesting." . . . But . . . you are a student, not a member of an audience.

A teacher is a special person, not to be confused with baby-sitter, repairman, psychoanalyst, or friend. If used properly, he will last a long time.

And adult students should not shy away from frank talks with teachers about these matters. Usually they [teachers] have reasons for what they do. . . . But anyone who has consented to teach has embarked upon an enterprise which can only be deemed successful if you as a student are satisfied. (Stern 1966, pp. 4–6)

My own experience as an instructor bears out the suggestion that instructors can be approached about what and how they teach. I must confess to having expected more of this than has been forthcoming. The infrequency with which most students avail themselves of opportunities for direct access and interchange has been disappointing. When I suggest that students drop by and chat about course content or processes, few take up the offer. For a long time I was prone to shoulder all the blame. Was I too forbidding or inaccessible? Did I put them down? The evidence seemed to say no. Perhaps rationalizing, I am now ready to conclude that students doubt that the offer is meant to be accepted; previous conditioning in the institutional setting has evidently left them prone to regard professors as givers of information much more than as resources for learning.

Concerning process, students may wish to (politely) ask an instructor about some of his or her assumptions concerning teaching and learning: "How would you describe your teaching style?" "Do you assume we all learn best in the same way?" Or, less adventuresome, "What are some keys to mastering this subject?" "Do you have any suggestions for my getting more from this course?" "Are your lectures largely supplemental to assigned text material?"

What are some other ways a learner can take active responsibility for learning in the classroom? One is to request an example when something is not understood. Another is to volunteer an example to confirm that something has been understood, bearing in mind that reluctance to speak in class is not unusual:

> When I first started back to college, I wouldn't say a word in class, not a word, through the whole meeting. No matter if I thought I had a wonderful idea. I wouldn't have presented it because you never know how they'll react to you. (Student quoted in Iazzetto 1980, p. 59)

Skillful learners can also relate what transpires in class to course goals and to personal learning purposes, and they seek clarification of unclear comments on papers returned to them.

Learning in the institutional setting can also be enhanced by increasing the learner's ability to profit from that methodological staple the lecture. A few commonly encountered tips include not relying on a tape recorder for taking notes (time may be wasted and active interaction with the information presented may be inhibited), reviewing notes frequently in order to foster insights and continuity, and having a note-taking system, such as that described by Jerold Apps (1978, p. 32). Apps suggests preparing notepaper in such a way as to facilitate the division of what is written into three categories: Key words, Notes, and Reflections and Conclusions.

Finally, when coming to grips with a new subject or discipline, it is useful for the learner to ask himself or herself questions such as these:

- How was this area of knowledge or practice developed?
- What are some of the basic concepts and terms?
- What are some of the key theories?
- Who are the most widely respected authorities?
- What are one or two recommended primers?

Writing Papers and Taking Exams

As most readers of this book will have had some experience in preparing research papers or essays in secondary school or college, I will not attempt here to provide detailed instructions for mastering what is obviously a complex process—one that involves critical thinking, organizing ideas, gathering information, and expressing oneself clearly in an academically acceptable format. Two books directed to adult students that are especially pertinent are Jerold Apps's *Study Skills for Those Adults Returning to School* (1978) and *Improve Your Writing Skills* (1982) and Cyril Houle's *Continuing Your Education* (1964). According to Martha Maxwell in *Improving Student Learning Skills* (1979), students have the most difficulties with following directions, locating good sources, clarity and coherence in expression, and systematic proofreading.

While attending schools and colleges—and when trying to get into them—people encounter a variety of devices and instruments designed to assess their potential and accomplishments. Among these are (1) the comprehensive examinations that govern admission to professional schools (for example, the Graduate Record Exam); (2) examinations that attempt to measure prior learning for placement or for credit; (3) end-of-course, certificate, or degree examinations; and (4) the tests and quizzes that routinely punctuate instruction. Testing also occurs in credit free situations—"before" and "after" tests, for example, in workshops and short courses. Written tests may take the form of the short answer (true-false, multiple choice, sentence completion) or the essay; they may be conducted in class (with or without student access to materials) or taken home. Oral exams are sometimes employed. And when skill achievement is the objective, competence may be demonstrated in other ways than by pencil and paper (e.g., by being observed in action or receiving a rating for objects one has produced). Whatever the purposes and the methodology, exams are almost always a source of anxiety.

Many instructors go out of their way to minimize the threat that testing potentially represents for adults and to build a climate in which the test represents a learning experience rather than a hurdle. They avoid tests with childish material; they sometimes allow students, with guidance, to have input into decisions about how, when, and where competence will be demonstrated. Students may even be permitted to test themselves. Some instructors limit testing to diagnostic purposes for helping to decide what materials and assignments to employ. Others coach students toward confidence and proficiency in testing situations. When confronted with less enlightened practices than these, certain tactics may prove useful.

Instructors can be asked about providing alternate ways for students to demonstrate what they have learned (contracts, peer reviews, action projects). Just as personal style comes into play in learning, it also is a factor in the verification that learning has occurred, and individuals usually have preferred ways of being evaluated. A learner can ask an instructor for suggestions for coping with the problems inherent in the testing instruments or methods to be used. Requesting criteria for good answers and for examples of them is usually in order. And a learner's decision whether to study alone, with others, or to use a combination of the two methods can be an important one that deserves careful thought.

Adults are usually aware of obvious suggestions such as "Don't rely on cramming," "Go over your paper carefully before you hand it in," "Get plenty of rest the night before," "Read the directions carefully."

All make good sense. The problem is to comply. Holding anxiety to an acceptable level can go a long way toward enabling compliance. Some tactics for controlling anxiety include expecting, and acknowledging, a certain amount of apprehension in testing situations. It is normal, showing that one is human and is involved. Try to avoid studying with people who overly resent the system or overly dramatize their own fears. Such persons can contribute to a learner's anxiety and siphon off time and energy.

Thus the person skilled in learning in educational institutions is acquainted with students' rights, knows how to use an instructor as a resource for learning, can assess the potential usefulness of a course or academic program, and is prepared to help instructors help him or her to learn in a manner that takes learning style into account. He or she can take useful notes, write papers, cope with exams, and meaningfully analyze a subject or discipline itself.

8

Some Alternative
Ways of Learning

In this chapter some alternative ways of learning are touched on. Three involve contemporary technology, while the others are perennials only now beginning to receive the attention of theorists and researchers. Advocates of these approaches often believe them to be as potentially useful as groups and classes are. None demands much in the way of financial outlay.

Learning Systematically from Everyday Experience

In *Rules for Radicals,* Saul Alinsky calls attention to the tendency of most people to react to life as "a series of happenings which pass through their systems undigested." His efforts to train community organizers led Alinsky to the conclusion that "happenings become experiences when they are digested, when they are reflected on, related to general patterns, and synthesized" (Alinsky 1972, pp. 68–69).

Poets and novelists have also called attention to the possibilities of learning from life experience. Dag Hammarskjöld said, "Let me read with open eyes the book . . . my days are writing—and learn." In *Mountolive,* the English writer Lawrence Durrell describes the heady experience of becoming immersed in another culture, saying of one of his characters, a European living in Egypt:

> Mountolive . . . suddenly began to feel himself really penetrating a foreign country, foreign *moeurs,* for the first time. He felt as one always feels in such a case, namely the vertiginous pleasure of losing an old self and growing a new one to replace it. He felt he was slipping, losing so to speak the contours of himself. Is this the real meaning of education? He

had begun transplanting a whole huge intact world from his imagination into the soil of his new life. (Durrell 1959, p. 21)

And the title of one of the great autobiographies, *The Education of Henry Adams,* reveals Adams's purpose to have been to draw educational implications from his life experience.

Adult educators enjoin us to learn from living and to help others do so. Malcolm Knowles (1975) speaks of the possibility of exploiting every experience as a learning experience. Virginia Griffin (1979) assigns high potential to personal experience, saying that principles derived by reflecting and conceptualizing from one's own experience are legitimate knowledge if they are thoughtfully and responsibly developed and tested.

It is evident that people do not necessarily place great value on their life experience. ("I've just been a housewife and mother.") Paulo Freire found Brazilian peasants ready to assume that literacy was not an appropriate goal for them because they believed that it went with "high culture" and being an important person. The peasants' lack of respect for their own life experience and resulting negative self-image had to be changed before they could be motivated to learn to read and write. Helping them to focus on that experience and on their world became the outside facilitator's central task (Freire 1974).

Saul Alinsky is not alone in pointing out that everyday experience does not necessarily accrue to the individual in desirable ways: "Experience may lead to wisdom or it may lead to dogmatism" (Sherron and Lumsden 1978, p. 31). The renowned psychologist B. F. Skinner calls experience "no school at all, not because no one learns in it, but because no one teaches" (Little 1979, p. 8).

It seems likely that, as people grow older, one obstacle to learning systematically from experience is the tendency to confuse what one has learned with what one has experienced. Harry Miller in his book *Teaching and Learning in Adult Education* identifies several others: the tendency to prejudge, an inability to attain the necessary objectivity to learn (when engaged in conversation, for example), the tendency to approach experience too passively, and the tendency of an individual to focus on differing and limited aspects of what is attended to (resulting in "differential interpretation of experience").

[A]ll of us learn poorly, lopsidedly, and wrongly from some experiences and not at all from others, because we do not know how to compensate for human frailties, how to frame the kinds of questions which can be asked about an experience to make it more meaningful, or how to look for connections and interrelationships which might be relevant to interpret experience. (Miller 1964, p. 230)

Learning to make relevant connections between experience and principles or concepts might be approached through a process of guided analysis of a local environment. People can participate in an election or walk through a neighborhood, for example, and then draw back and reflect about what they have learned. The role of the guide, or trainer, is to make the experiences focuses for learning about learning from experience.

> [T]he objective is not that they learn something [in particular] about [say] a political campaign but that they discover what questions need to be asked, how one overcomes one's own preconceptions, what kinds of inferences may be safely made in a given situation, and the habit of thoughtful reflection. (Miller 1964, p. 232)

Lacking a guide, one might approach the development of improved skills in learning from experience by preplanning for an upcoming episode or period. Faced with a month of active military service, a stint as a volunteer, jury duty, or caring for an invalid, one can mull over the potential opportunities for learning—learning about organizations, justice, or human relationships. It should be useful to ask and write down such questions as, What personal assumptions can be tested? and What biases do I bring to the endeavor? Later the products of such planning can serve as a basis for analyzing what has transpired, and perhaps mean the difference between piling up experience and learning from it. One may come to digest the happenings that pass through the system.

Many persons use diaries or journals as a means to learning from experience. In addition to specific events, they record thoughts, questions, insights, quotations, and shifts in interests, points of view, or values. Workshops concerning journal keeping as a tool for personal growth appear to be proliferating (Simons 1978).

Reminiscing is an almost universal technique for extracting meaning from experience. At least this constitutes one of its functions; others include coping and providing a means of self-expression. For the elderly, reminiscing has been found to be associated with more positive attitudes toward their pasts and deriving a sense of integrity and purpose in life (Merriam and Cross, in press).

Old age obviously presents a vantage point from which to derive meaning from the environment, to create perspectives, and to sum up. Exploring one's past and the events in which it is imbedded can lead to understanding through the discovery of some things that are timeless: "Each single human life can become a microcosm for all generations" (Sherron and Lumsden 1978). Thus people often search for their roots as a means of interpreting their own lives; when this occurs, reminiscing becomes interwoven with learning new material.

Learning from Mentors

A mentor is like a resource person available for relatively long periods of time—the first several years one is in a job or in a volunteer service role, for example. More often than not the relationship evolves naturally rather than through the kind of deliberate contracting that an apprenticeship or an internship involves. The effects of, and the potential of, using mentors for learning is increasingly coming under examination and research (Bolton 1980).

Mentors do more than help people to learn and solve problems. They provide role models for others (often serving to raise aspirations), they actively encourage learners, and they often act as advocates. But the learning dimension of the relationship is usually a critical one. It is also the aspect over which the learner has the most control. Although one does not demand that another serve as mentor, one can try to learn effectively when a mentor comes along.

Like a parent with a child, a mentor may provide support and protection. The support and protection may be especially helpful when coming to understand a new environment and one's role in it—how things are done and get done. The learner may be helped to identify sources of persistent problems. Help in handling success can be forthcoming as well as a bit of consolation at times. Naiveté and lack of realism can be gently but firmly pointed out.

Like any good resource person, the ideal mentor listens, asks questions, and occasionally makes suggestions. He or she also resists certain temptations such as looking at a learner as a possession to be made over in his or her own image or permitting more dependency or intimacy than is constructive. Usually the most successful mentors have themselves benefited from experience as learners.

Women have less chance than men of establishing a successful relationship with a mentor, especially in the business and professional work setting. Since on the whole fewer women than men have risen to managerial and leadership positions, women usually have few members of their own sex to draw on. And the danger that motives may be misunderstood often discourages males from serving as mentors for females.

How can one go about trying to establish a successful relationship with a mentor? While mentors aren't for hire, a relationship with one is most likely to come about through such actions as attending professional meetings, analyzing the potential help in a work or service setting, and asking individuals for assistance when it is genuinely needed. Locating a mentor outside one's own organization can be helpful for political reasons—forestalling charges of favoritism or suspicion of motive, for example.

To get the most from a mentor, one must be willing to ask for help sometimes. It is essential to do more than observe, and one needs to take what is personally useful and appropriate from the mentor. Merely copying the other person's behavior and style won't do. When mentors are not being helpful, they deserve to know it, and when their advice is not taken, they appreciate an explanation.

It is to be expected that the relationship will change, develop, and probably decline after a time, since dependency should gradually decrease. Outgrowing the need for a mentor is natural, and it is realistic to expect some pain or difficulty when the relationship becomes less intense or terminates.

It's nice to let mentors know, even many years later, that their help is appreciated. As one grows older, such a gift may become more important than a material one.

Learning from Television and Radio

The mass media of television and radio obviously have the power to exert strong effects on values and attitudes as they simultaneously present information, entertainment, and distraction: "Television and radio producers are de facto educators" (Botkin et al. 1979, p. 99).

Public television and radio offer a variety of programming that is either educational in intent or of sufficiently high aesthetic standards to gladden the hearts of those of us who like to think of ourselves as discriminating. To learn a considerable amount from many of the programs, one needs to do little more than pay attention. Follow-up reading or trips to museums, galleries, and live performances can enrich the viewing or listening experience.

Some public television and radio programs, and occasionally one on commercial television, are produced with accompanying reading material. The trick is to be alert enough to know in advance what is coming and how to obtain the materials; such information is usually available from the stations themselves and from public libraries. About 75 percent of the public television stations also broadcast credit and noncredit postsecondary education courses.

Radio is often overlooked as a source for learning, perhaps because of the compelling power of television, perhaps because radio tends to be taken for granted and used as a background for doing something else. The rural population has received useful information for half a century via the broadcasts of the Cooperative Extension Service. Public radio today treats a wide variety of issues in some depth and presents a great deal of serious music and opera. The automobile tape cassette has opened possibilities for learning on the move by means of programming available from educational entrepreneurs.

Gleaning the most learning from mass media requires approaching the art of listening and viewing in much the same way that the skilled reader usually approaches a book—actively and critically. Self-raised questions can be helpful: What information is being left out? What information appears slanted? What do the broadcasters wish to be believed or accepted? What assumptions are the arguments based on? What themes can be found in the material? What concepts still confuse and beg clarification?

The preplanning of viewing and listening is essential for this kind of learning. Scanning a program guide and selecting one or two promising shows and noting them on the calendar can be done on Sunday as one puts aside the newspapers and thinks about the coming week. There are at least two ways to build the structure lacking in most media offerings. One is to form an informal listening or viewing group in which people share their reactions to what is presented. The other is to construct a personal learning project (around, say, an upcoming series of programs on investments; the program content can be supplemented and made meaningful by means of written materials obtained from libraries or banks and consultation with friends and experts).

A comprehensive program for training adults to learn more effectively through television has been developed at Boston University's School for Public Communication under a grant from the federal government. Called "Critical Television Viewing Skills," the program consists of modular materials in these four areas: television literacy, persuasive programming, entertainment programming, and informational programming.

Learning with Computers

Adult learners and adult educators are increasingly making use of computer technology. Computer-assisted instruction (CAI) is proving useful in such diverse areas as basic education, continuing medical education, and employee education. Information retrieval systems (e.g., the Educational Resources Information Centers) can be used to scan rapidly vast quantities of research-related material. And, together with electronic games, home computers offer a wide range of possibilities for learning.

Like those who heralded the earlier contributions to technology—

the printing press, radio, television, audio and video recorders and players—some enthusiasts are now heralding learning by computer as the ultimate weapon in the battle against ignorance. While it hardly seems likely that such prospects are in store given the complexities of humans and of learning, the computer obviously constitutes another quite useful resource when appropriately used.

Adults seeking to take advantage of computer learning need to bear in mind the difference between computer-assisted instruction and computer-managed instruction. CAI represents a computer-video display terminal system that incorporates programmed instructional materials. It is typically used to supplement other kinds of instruction in the classroom and laboratory. The system can aid in diagnosing educational needs, presenting information, monitoring progress, and providing feedback to both students and instructors. One three-year study terms CAI an "ideal supplementary medium for adults" (Buckley 1979, p. 5a). With computer-managed instruction, the idea is to place the computer in control of the total instructional process. In this instance, rather than supplementing other forms of instruction, the computer more or less can substitute for the instructor. The total instructional package for which the computer serves as the brain and nervous system often includes other audiovisual materials and some printed matter like workbooks. Perhaps the best-known system for computer-managed instruction, called PLATO, was developed over a decade ago at the University of Illinois and marketed by Control Data Corporation.

A growing number of educational agencies are offering training for learning by computer. The best of these offerings aim not only at so-called computer awareness but also at skill in using computers for purposes of instruction and the carrying out of learning projects. They include provision for trainees to write and modify programs. The knowledgeable consumer will look for generous amounts of hands-on experience (Billings and Moursund 1979; Luehrmann 1980). Finally, training for successful use of such information-retrieval systems as ERIC and DATRIX can usually be obtained through colleges and universities, often at little or no cost to the trainee.

Learning Through Intuition and Dreams

It was mentioned in chapter 2 that learning has its intuitive side. The possibilities of intuitive learning are intriguing. Intuition has been called a source of direct information about reality. Most people would agree that insights and problem solving and growth are not brought about through words alone, and many feel that intuitive learning will receive increasing attention from researchers and practitioners in the future (Roberts 1975).

In recognition of the importance of the subjective side of learning, teachers of children and youth are also being urged to turn their attention to the processes that control inner states, so-called transpersonal processes. Frances Clark explains these processes as ones in which learning is not geared to the acquisition or transmission of information, but to "participation in the process of unfolding from within." But techniques devised for eliciting transpersonal experience do not automatically lead to the awakening of transpersonal awareness. The process is rather one of "getting out of the way." As the desired insights are to be discovered from within, all the teacher can do is create the appropriate situation. One way of facilitating the process is to allow students to share subjective experiences with others.

Clark describes an example of training for the development of intuition. Two persons, who preferably do not know each other, sit facing each other; they are instructed to relax and quiet their minds, and then, in silence, to notice (but not to interpret) any thoughts or feelings that come to their awareness as they attend to each other. They note images—visual, auditory, or kinesthetic—that arise or are induced through such questions as, "If she were a light, what color or intensity would it be? What type of sound would she be?" After a time the two people share their impressions in a nonjudgmental way. However, interpretation is secondary to prevent its inhibiting the spontaneous flow of imagery (Clark 1975).

Margaret Denis, an adult educator, has developed a model of intuitive learning from in-depth interviews with twenty-five persons and a personal experiment. The processes she describes are of a different order of things than activities, sequential steps, methods, or techniques. They are "energies, each with their own dynamic, influencing in their own way the intuitive process of learning." Each process goes on in the learner at some level of awareness throughout an intuitive learning episode; most occur simultaneously or with a high degree of overlap or interrelationship. Denis's interesting venture into uncharted areas shows potential for helping us to understand and to increase skills needed for intuitive learning.

Dreams can be seen as kinds of metaphors into which information is compressed. Sharing dreams with others is a key technique employed by some adults who use dreams for growth and change. One study of forty such persons found dreams to be a way for them to get in touch with their innermost being and to articulate feelings in picture form. These subjects used dreams and subsequent reflective activity as a basis for making major decisions; decisions tended to be in the area of values and spiritual matters. Improved psychological functioning was frequently reported. The specific kinds of process help that the subjects expressed interest in were as follows: (1) handling conflict dreams, (2) making dreams clearer, (3) understanding why periods of dormancy occur when things are going well, (4) assistance in quickly recalling a dream after awakening, (5) understanding why dreams sometimes occur in serialized episodes, and (6) forming a contact network with other persons who take dreams seriously (Thomas 1978).

Some so-called primitive cultures continue to show the high respect for dreams that sources like the Old Testament indicate was once more widespread. Dream interpretation is at the very center of the lives of the Senoi people in Malaysia—a people exhibiting relatively little mental illness. Families begin the day discussing members' dreams from the night before. The British anthropologist Kilton Stewart believes that the Senoi's system of dream interpretation is directly related to what he calls their successful psychosocial system (Kantor 1974).

Other nonrational approaches to learning about which there is currently considerable interest include learning from the future, which uses such techniques as imagining one's memoirs (Botkin 1979), learning through fantasy and guided daydreams (Clark 1975), learning while sleeping (a foreign language, for example), and the "suggestology" approach of the Bulgarian psychiatrist Georgi Lozanov (Ostrander and Schroeder 1979). A source of further information about subjective ways of learning and their required skills is The Association for Humanistic Psychology, 325 Ninth Street, San Francisco, CA 94103.

Part III

Providing Training: Helping Others Learn How to Learn

We turn now to the third component of the learning how to learn concept—training. Training was defined earlier as organized activity to increase people's competence in learning and to help them to become more successful in the realm of education. The way in which training and learning style relate to the development of skill in learning (to learners' needs and competencies concerning learning itself) was explained in chapter 1. In Part II some practical implications of the learning how to learn concept from the point of view of the learner were set forth. These final two chapters are meant for adult educators who wish to implement the learning how to learn concept with their clients. It should be clear that much of the information contained in earlier chapters (and the appendixes) becomes resource material for the designing and conducting of training.

9

Guidelines for Training

---

*Give a man a fish and he eats for a day. Teach him to fish
and he eats for a lifetime.*

Proverb

Teaching people how to learn enables education to nourish them. We
call instruction of this kind *training* and use the term, despite certain
drawbacks, because it has a history of such a usage and because it is
the best of the available options. (Compare this unwieldy alternative:
"arranging for learning about education and learning.") The term
training permits us to communicate with some precision about a central aspect of learning how to learn. The way in which training relates
to the development of skill in learning and to learning style—the third
component of the learning how to learn concept—was explained in
chapter 1.

Training efforts have the best chances for success when one can
apply a bit of theory and visualize what is involved in the design of
activities. It is often necessary to sell training—to convince others of
its importance—and to improvise designs, exercises, and materials.
These kinds of activities usually require sensitivity, self-awareness,
and willingness to experiment on the part of the adult educator. They
may entail some frustration. But the rewards justify the effort. Like
baseball pitchers who take pride in their success when batting, many
educators have come to derive exceptional satisfaction from the provision of useful training for their clients. For example, Malcolm Knowles
(1980b) reports that teachers who have helped adult students to ac-

cept major responsibility for their own learning find it to be one of the most rewarding experiences of their lives.

Training can be directed at improved effectiveness in self-directed learning, collaborative learning, or institutional learning. Activities are characteristically carried out in one of three ways. The first is the module or episode that constitutes the initial phase of a longer educational experience. For example, opening sessions in a course that will emphasize discussion may be devoted to training the participants in discussion skills, or a seminar to be based on student research and reports may begin with training in how to do the particular type of research in question and how to prepare and deliver an effective report. The second is to build in training throughout a learning experience—as when each class session is concluded with a critique concerning its usefulness and consideration of ways for the participants to learn more effectively in future sessions. And the third is a separate training event. Examples might be a laboratory concerning the learning how to learn concept itself, a course in study skills, the participation training institute (McKinley 1978), or a workshop devoted to more effective conduct of personal learning projects.

Concerning the selling, or justification, of training, the question arises as to whether or not adults will react positively when the idea of training is broached. How will someone who is ready to learn a subject or skill react to the idea of preparing to learn it in a certain way— marking time before the "real learning" gets under way? Experience shows that people find training acceptable when it (1) has the possibility of a larger payoff (e.g., acquiring skills that can be used in comparable situations) and (2) clearly relates to previously encountered learning problems (e.g., apathetic groups, aborted personal learning projects, or exam anxiety).

Training Design

One trusted axiom of adult educators—"Involve the participant in the planning process"—is best forgotten when designing training activities. Training design is an exception. In this instance, the planning process is sufficiently complex—involving learning about learning—to preclude much useful input from the participant. To be sure, the latter can provide useful feedback as to the effectiveness of training. And, when training is conducted, people can make useful process contributions—for example, when they are given the opportunity to identify characteristics of their own learning styles or asked to describe previous learning situations found to be distressing or satisfying.

The main reason participants should not be involved in training design is that few if any will feel at home with the kind of multilevel diagnosis that is usually required. When people are asked to practice a certain behavior related to improved learning skill—to lead a discussion, to plan and conduct a personal learning project, or to study a book instead of merely reading it—and then to step back and analyze what was done, they typically have difficulty in distinguishing *what* was done from *how* it was done. To invite them to help design training, which introduces a third level of complexity, is not realistic.

Training designers therefore try to think as clearly as they can about objectives, suitability of exercises, and the preparation of people for training experiences. They often build in as much time for analysis or critique—for helping trainees to externalize and then internalize the learning about learning implications of an activity—as for the conducting of the activity itself.

Training should usually be designed so as to approximate as closely as possible the conditions under which what is being learned about learning will be put to use. This means that role play and simulation are often employed. It also means emphasis on doing—developing planning skills by planning something and skills for conducting learning activities by conducting them in a practice environment. There should also be included some provision for gaining insight into any differences between the simulated or actual conditions experienced in the training situation and the anticipated situations to be encountered "back home" or wherever the skills and understandings are to be used. The development of realistic plans and images of future use fosters the transfer of training.

It is important to avoid the temptation to overload a training resource or exercise. A sample plan for a personal learning project that deals with the subject of self-directed learning itself will probably confuse the reader. A practice exercise for improving discussion skills that requires people to discuss what makes for good discussion also introduces an unnecessary complication. And to allow a training group to try to plan a program about program planning can mean the sanctioning of unusual punishment.

A Change Process

Trainers challenge or gently force trainees to look at their assumptions and behavior concerning such matters as authority and need for structure, what learning is, and the teaching-learning process (Knowles 1975; Gibbs 1981). Trainees learn about learning as they become open to change in a climate of trust initiated by the trainer and then jointly maintained by both (Thomas and Harri-Augstein 1977).

Conflict →	Defense →	Resolution of the Conflict →	Incorporation
Learner feels need for change, yet wishes to remain as is when faced with information that threatens his/her present attitudes and behavior. This ambivalence is a conflict between "the old" and "the new." It creates tension in the learner and a desire to resolve the conflict.	Learner defends self against ideas that require admitting personal limitations and resists the will of someone else or something to change him/her. Defense involves *projection*—we defend our present ideas by asserting ourselves as we now are, by blaming somebody or some circumstances—and *rationalization*—we become angry, we withdraw, or we don't listen actively, in order to protect ourselves.	Learner struggles with self—the new way vs. habitual ways. Ideally, the original ambivalence is examined objectively. The learner must make the decision to change. The learner is free to face the ambivalence within himself/herself (1) when no one insists on changing him/her; (2) when he/she can express self freely; (3) when he/she feels accepted regardless of attitude; (4) when not attacked or put on the defensive. The process of incorporation is often aided by *identification* with others.	Learner understands, accepts, and assimilates the new.
When the need for change is readily apparent, learners sometimes resolve this conflict by passing rapidly to steps 3 and 4.			

Fig. 12. A Pattern of Learning That Leads to Change

Since training usually represents deliberate efforts to change behavior, it often requires "unlearning." The trainer needs to understand that the change process generally goes something like this: an awareness of the need for change; an unfreezing or loosening up with regard to assumptions about learning and behavior; dealing with need to change in positive ways so as to move in preferred directions; and an integration or consolidation of change (incorporation of new behavior) and refreezing.

Experienced trainers expect some resistance, even hostility. People do not necessarily like to have their inability to listen or dysfunctional study practices brought to the fore. And people do not usually change habits or basic orientations to learning without some conflict or frustration. When conflict and frustration occur, they may well be directed against the nearest available target—the trainer.

Another way of describing the change process that learners, in this instance trainees, often experience has been suggested (see figure 12).

Trainers also need the discipline to avoid being seduced by content, since processes are what they are trying to help learners to focus on. Harry Miller (1964) describes this phenomenon in connection with training people to learn more effectively from everyday experience. John McKinley (1978) warns the participation trainer against becoming fascinated by, or overly involved in, the content of the discussion exercises that people undergo in participation training.

When the lack of an appropriate resource or design dictates improvisation, the trainer can either adapt an already existing one or seek to invent one. For example, many of the more than 300 exercises in the annual handbook series edited by J. William Pfeiffer and John E. Jones may be adapted for training centered in learning-skills improvement. The way in which one instructor devised a means to renew motivation by helping students understand the learning plateau concept is described by Jennifer Rogers (1971). And a videotape developed by the Maryland Department of Education (1975) for preservice and inservice education of adult basic education instructors shows how an instructor improvises ways to get students to improve the ability to recall specific information.

A word about the training of trainers is in order. Perhaps the development of trainers is a preferable expression, for experience has shown that there is no royal road to producing trainers. The task is best understood as a process, since training trainer courses have seldom proven productive. When an extensive training design is involved, the process usually involves four stages: the person first experiences the activity in question in a training situation; the trainee then applies the training "back home"; the trainee serves as assistant or helping trainer in a training situation; and, finally, the trainee conducts training activities independently. Evaluation and certification as a trainer may or may not be interposed between steps three and four as has been done, for example, by the National Training Laboratories and Indiana University in laboratory training and participation training, respectively. However, training skill for the kinds of purposes described in chapter 10 can be developed on one's own through experimentation and clues from printed resources.

It should be clear that developing competence in the trainer role involves making the idea of training understandable and palatable, creating a climate that fosters behavioral change, thinking clearly about the design of activities, being able to distinguish content from process, locating or improvising training resources and exercises, dealing constructively with resistance, heightening the trainee's awareness of self as learner and the sensitivity to learning itself, and adopting an experimental, learn as we go, frame of mind.

Additional training theory is found in chapter 10 embedded in applications for helping people learn to learn more effectively on their own, in collaborative groups, and through educational institutions.

10

Training Designs
and Activities

This chapter treats ways of deliberately helping others to take advantage of education and to learn more effectively—on their own, in collaborative groups, and through educational institutions. Such activity constitutes training, although those responsible may not refer to it as such or to themselves as trainers when they engage in it.

Training for Self-directed Learning

In order to move directly from theory to practice a training design will be presented. It has been developed and tested by the author in twelve workshops over a six-year period; it is meant to serve as an example of an introductory training experience for providing knowledge and skill for learning in this mode. As such it serves much the same function as participation training does for collaborative learning and the in-depth learning how to learn course offered in a few colleges here and abroad (McKinley 1978 and 1980; Gibbs 1981).

Workshop on Self-directed Learning

Overall Workshop Goals and Purposes

Increased understanding of self as learner and self-directed learning

Increased skill in planning, conducting, and evaluating a personal learning project

Resources for the Trainer

The Lifelong Learner by Ronald Gross

Self-Directed Learning by Malcolm Knowles
The Adult's Learning Projects by Allen M. Tough
Chapters 5 and 9 of this book (When not otherwise designated, citations are in this book.)

Number of Contact Hours

12 (+ or −)

Optimum Number of Participants

12–24

Training Staff

Director; assistant trainer if group is larger than 15

Facilities

Informal, movable chairs and tables; retreat setting if feasible

Preworkshop Reading Assignment for Participants (Trainees)

The Lifelong Learner, especially chapters 1 and 2
Chapter 4
Chapter 5

Module I

Objectives

To encourage trainee awareness of self as learner
To establish that the identification and analysis of learning processes can be interesting and productive

Possible Topics for Theory Presentation

What research says about personal learning projects—their nature, extent, and uses
Some requirements for successful projects
The development of a plan for a project

Resources

Thinking About Learning Exercise (Appendix D)
Sample learning plans, chapter 5, pp. 96–97

Format

Time in Minutes	Activity
20	Introduction and orientation to workshop
80	Thinking About Learning Exercise (Appendix D)
15	Break
25	Theory presentation
20	Further orientation and clarification of activities and responsibilities for remainder of workshop (Participants will carry out a personal learning project between Module II and Module IV. This activity will be processed during Module IV.)

Assignment

Develop a plan for a learning project. Bring two copies to the
next meeting.
Read *Self-Directed Learning,* Part I; chapter 4, pp. 84–90

Module II

Objectives

To introduce the learning-style concept and assist participants
to gain a perspective on their own learning styles
To prepare participants to carry out and analyze a personal
learning project

Possible Topics for Theory Presentation

The learning-style concept and its implications for self-directed
learning
Problems to anticipate in carrying out a personal learning
project

Resources

The plan for a learning project brought by each participant
Multiple copies of at least one learning-style instrument
"Learning: A Matter of Style," 25–minute color videotape
(Dunn 1979)

Format

Time in Minutes	Activity
5	Review and orientation to Module II
55	Style profiling exercise and discussion of results
15	Break
30	Theory presentation or viewing of the videotape
60	Consultations with individuals concerning their plans for learning projects
15	Consolidating of training thus far about learning, about learning style, about learning on your own, and about the carrying out of learning projects

Assignment

Conduct your learning project

Write a short paper (about 500 words) describing it and setting forth what you learned about self as learner and about this kind of learning (due at Module IV). Concentrate on *process*. Devote no more than 20 percent of the paper to *what* you did.

Read *The Lifelong Learner,* chapter 5; chapter 5, pp. 100–05

Module III

Objectives

To provide information useful to trainees in conducting their personal learning projects and in meaningfully analyzing them

To increase skill in using resource persons on a one-to-one basis

Possible Topics for Theory Presentation

How to monitor your learning project while it is going on (e.g., keep a log)

How to use resource persons on a one-to-one basis

Getting useful feedback when learning this way

Resources

Learning from a Resource Person Exercise (Appendix E)

Format

Time in Minutes	Activity
10	Review and orientation to Module III
60	Learning from a Resource Person Exercise (Appendix E)
15	Break
30	Clinical session—trainer-led discussion: "What Problems Are You Encountering with Your Projects?"
60	Theory presentation, individual consultation, or peer consultation concerning progress and problems with projects and with assignment made at Module II

Module IV

Objectives

To extract relevant process learnings from the project each
person conducted
To synthesize what has been learned about self-directed learning
and to encourage postworkshop application of the training

Resources

The plans that participants developed between Modules I and II
Reports by participants of personal learning projects and their
analysis of same

Format

Time in Minutes	Activity
15	Recap of what the workshop has been concerned with and the intended outcomes Orientation to Module IV
60–90	In general session or in groups of 8–12 with a trainer in each, trainees report on their projects and the insights gained; trainer leads group in a brief critique after each report

15	Break
30	Applying what has been learned about self-directed learning (small groups devise ways)
15	Feedback to trainer for improvement of future training activities
	(Trainer usually reads the written reports after the workshop and returns them by mail with comments.)

This design for a separate event concerning self-directed learning illustrates some general characteristics of training in the context of learning how to learn.

Goals and objectives should be relatively modest, carefully thought through, and clearly stated. The extent to which they are shared with trainees will vary from trainer to trainer and situation to situation.

Activities are a blend of theory and actual or simulated practice. Theory should be kept to a minimum and brought to bear on experience. Training exercises are often provided in advance of theory presentations. Rather than telling, the trainer seeks to create conditions under which people examine present assumptions and ways of doing things and substitute better ways (in this case to direct their own learning and carry out personal learning projects).

Designs and resources developed by others usually have to be adapted to the trainer's own needs and purposes. When modifying a training design or an exercise, trainers take into account group size, physical environment, and the previous experience of trainees (e.g., the frequency with which they normally conduct personal learning projects). An example of adapting the same design would be to devise a training event of about six hours with comparable but more limited objectives, one that did not include the carrying out of a personal learning project between modules. Simulation and case studies might be employed. The training exercises and the videotape might be used along with learning-style profiling and the sample learning plans found in chapter 5, pp. 96–97. Each participant might develop and have critiqued one or more plans for later implementation or undertake analysis of past personal learning projects.

Special Considerations in Training for Self-directed Learning

Motivation. Trainees may be less ready to recognize the need for improvement in the directing of their own learning than for learning collaboratively or for learning in the classroom. They tend to be unaware of the range and scope of personal projects they habitually carry out. The idea of self-directed learning as an improvable process may seem harder to grasp than is the case with small-group performance or the relevance of study-skills training for success in school or college. The formidable evidence compiled through the research of Allen Tough and his associates can be used to demonstrate the ubiquity of this kind of learning, its characteristics, and problems; the enthusiasm and force of a skilled writer like Ronald Gross can contribute to a positive frame of mind. But for the training to take, activities will need to be arranged that demonstrate the value of examining how one goes about learning on one's own. Two activities that have proven especially effective are profiling personal learning style and critiquing (by self, peers, and trainers) actual learning projects.

Focus on Process.   The trainer seeks to establish a safe climate and help the trainee attend to how he or she goes about learning in the self-directed mode. But when people describe or react to the learning-related aspects of experience, they are prone to focus on such matters as what they did and to mistake description for analysis. They have difficulty staying with the implications for improved learning or insights into the self as a learner in this mode. Most trainees asked for the first time to present a short oral or written report that analyzes a learning project need guidance if they are to avoid devoting the bulk of their presentation to content rather than process. The trainer tries to foster a process orientation in the trainee by providing appropriate directions in bridging activities, exercises, and assignments; by modeling diagnostic behavior (e.g., asking such questions as, "What was the effect of using your mother as a resource person?" "What might have been a way around the problem of too many books being available on your topic?"); and by making theory presentations that reiterate the need for trainees to come to see process as the important content of training and help trainees learn to deal simultaneously with the content-process dimensions of experience.

Although trainers themselves must avoid "content seduction," they usually find it useful to take into account people's basic orientation toward content when designing, promoting, and conducting training activities. Thus a workshop on self-directed learning might be held in a public library and mix in some time for browsing in library materials with exercises like those in the sample design. A workshop might be better billed, for example, as "Bright Ideas for Learning" than "Becoming a Self-directed Learner." I have used successfully the former title for such a workshop; in addition to training exercises the participants received materials, prepared by the library staff, concerning "What to Learn About," and "Where to Learn" (local area educational opportunities), and "Resources About Adult Learning" (i.e., an annotated bibliography of self-help books). Some participants proved to be especially interested in the suggestions for subject matter, while others preferred the process skills training.

Another tip is to avoid making this kind of training overly rigorous or technical. There should be room for creativity and spontaneity in conducting learning projects. (Some people even respond negatively to the term *project*.) The trainer needs to be able to accommodate to the serendipitous learner as well as to the one who can be intrigued with the idea of drawing up a contract.

The Locus.   Training for self-directed learning need not be done in groups. Coaching, tutoring, or counseling—call it what you like—can be at least as effective. However, one-to-one approaches make sufficiently large demands on trainer time and energy as to discourage their use by educational agencies and such individual providers of training as classroom instructors. Training for collaborative learning— our next topic—offers no option, since it is almost impossible to foster the necessary skills in anything but a group setting.

Training for Collaborative Learning

The broad goals of training for this kind of learning can be described as improved group membership skills and teamwork development. Training involves helping people to understand the conditions under which adults learn best in face-to-face groups, helping people learn how to learn with and from one another while using other resources as needed, and fostering the development of diagnostic skills and the ability to distinguish content from process. Trainees can learn how to share in program development—in the planning, conducting, and evaluating of their own group learning and problem-solving activities. More specifically, training should be directed toward improved communication, increased ability to give and receive feedback, better performance in the leadership role, increased skill in planning, and better consensus decision-making.

In chapter 6 both the effective collaborative learning group and a dysfunctional one were described. Suggestions for carrying out the roles of leader and participant and a tested planning procedure were presented, and some training sources were identified.

Comprehensive training experiences—such as the week-long Participation Training Institute and some of those associated with the National Training Laboratory—may be aimed at all of the goals and objectives training should be directed toward. (Bradford 1964; Benne 1975; Knowles and Knowles 1972; McKinley 1978; McKenzie 1975; Smith 1969). The training is often conducted in a retreat setting with several staff members providing theory and practice sessions for twenty to forty persons. Much of the time is spent in groups of ten to fifteen persons, each of which has at least one trainer assigned to it. The trainees implement activities designed to illustrate theory, improve skills, and provide a common experience-base for analysis and consolidation of learnings related to group learning itself. In the celebrated T-group of laboratory training, the trainees are "agendaless," being assigned the task of "interacting" and "becoming a group" (Benne 1975). In participation training, group members employ two formats for structuring of activity. One is called Topic, Goals, and Outline. The other is the six-step planning procedure described in chapter 6 (McKinley 1978; Bergevin, Morris, and Smith 1963).

Activities and Exercises
for Collaborative Learning

For Improving Communication.   Training for this objective aims at getting people to listen more actively, to become more sensitive to nonverbal cues, and to learn to help one another to be understood. Various combinations of theory and activity can be used. Merely concluding a regularly scheduled session with a ten-minute discussion of questions such as these can be helpful: What communication barriers have we noticed? Is there jargon and technical language? Do people talk past each other? Are several conversations going at once? What can we do to improve communication?

Activities

1. Ask for a volunteer to serve as an observer for the upcoming session. The observer sits outside the group and watches what goes on. The idea is to record some information that might prove useful to the group in diagnosing obstacles to communication. In a short verbal report the observer can deal with such matters as patterns of verbal interaction (by charting who speaks to whom) and symptoms of people not being heard or understood.

   Be sure that the observer sticks to what he or she observed, tries to stay away from content, avoids judgments, and does not mention people's names without prior group approval to do so.

Lead a period of analysis, or critique, in which the group members confirm the accuracy and explore the implications of the information presented by the observer.

Alternative:
Trainer models the observer role and asks group members to be responsible for reacting to the data offered them.

2. Divide the group, if it is larger than ten persons, into subgroups of six to nine members. Assign a topic that can be discussed meaningfully for about fifteen minutes (e.g., "How could our organization get more members?" "How could nursing staff–medical staff relations be improved?").

    Ask the group(s) to discuss the topic without a designated leader. Impose one condition: each time a group member speaks he or she must give a brief summary of the remarks made by the person who has just spoken. The summary should be acceptable to the previous speaker.

    Conclude with a trainer-led analysis of insights gained and implications for improved listening.

3. Divide the group and assign a topic as in the second activity. Have one or two persons (volunteers) in each group observe the discussion, focusing on nonverbal communication such as signs of interest or disinterest, posture and eye contact, supportive behavior, and uncomfortable silences.

    Discontinue the discussion after about fifteen minutes and ask the group(s) to analyze their process and progress in terms of information presented in a short report by the observer(s).

Additional Materials

McKinley, *Participants Manual,* pp. 15, 23–26
Pfeiffer and Jones, Vols. I, II, and IV
Chapter 6

For Giving and Receiving Feedback.   Training for this objective is directed toward encouraging people to share their perceptions of what happens in the group and how individual and group behavior affect the individual's learning and progress toward group goals. Training involves establishing a climate in which people feel safe enough to open up a bit to reveal some feelings and ask for help, and legitimizing the giving and receiving of feedback.

Feedback is most acceptable and useful when it is solicited by the person receiving it, when it comes from trusted persons, when it is descriptive and related to a specific situation, and when character and personality are not judged or indicted.

Trainers can themselves model behavior that invites feedback, asking, for example, "Is this training useful?" This can be done openly or, until trust levels become high, by requesting unsigned written reactions after an activity or session.

Activities

1. Use the Requesting Feedback Exercise (Appendix C). Make copies for each person. Follow the exercise with discussion of what has been learned about the giving and receiving of feedback and the implications for future sessions. (Takes about forty-five minutes.)

2. When trust levels have become high, conclude a regularly scheduled session with a brief period in which individuals are offered the opportunity to request personal feedback about how they might have helped others to learn more effectively.

3. For a group whose members have come to know one another reasonably well and when some positive feedback is in order, give each member as many slips of paper as he or she will need to write a positive message to each member of the group.

   Encourage the trainees to make their messages brief, specific, and personalized. Messages are written, "addressed," and placed where the recipient has designated.

   After messages have been read (silently), the trainees may share what they've learned about themselves or found most helpful (but no pressure to do so should be exerted).

Additional Materials

Kidd, *How Adults Learn,* pp. 287–89
McKinley, *Participants Manual,* p. 14
McKinley, *Trainer's Resource,* pp. 28–30
Pfeiffer and Jones, Vols. I and III
Chapter 6

For Improving Leadership.   Ideally a collaborative learning group would not require a great deal of overt leadership by a designated leader or chairperson. The members would be able to lead themselves as a result of having come to accept responsibility for progress toward goals and for helping one another to learn. But more realistically it is often desirable to provide training concerning such tasks as climate setting, arranging the physical environment, introducing a topic or problem, questioning, keeping specific goal(s) before the group, and summarizing.

Activity

For groups of eight to fourteen persons, hold a series of thirty- to forty-minute discussions on topics chosen by the group itself, each led by a different (volunteer) leader who wishes to improve his or her leadership skills.

Critique each leader's performance in terms of the guidelines in chapter 6, pp. 109–10. Open the analysis with an opportunity for the person who has just served as leader to speak first to identify his or her own strengths and shortcomings and to tell how he or she felt in the role.

Additional Materials

McKinley, *Participants Manual*, p. 12
Chapter 6

For More Effective Planning. Training aims at (1) fostering the idea that planning is learning; (2) demonstrating that increased motivation results from learners sharing in program development (deciding what and how they will learn and be evaluated); and (3) providing guided planning experience in which educational needs, interests, and goals are identified before resources and procedures are selected.

Activities

1. For a group of fourteen to twenty-four persons, divide the trainees into two subgroups and have each subgroup simultaneously plan a one-hour learning activity that will involve the total group when it is conducted. Groups should use the six-step planning procedure described in chapter 6, pp. 112–15. (This activity takes about five hours altogether.)

   After each of the programs is conducted, the trainer leads a critique with the guidelines found in the Collaborative Learning Appraisal Form (Appendix J).

2. A variation of the first activity is one in which groups plan programs but do not conduct them. The process and the product of the planning are critiqued. Each group presents, through one or more spokespersons, its format and goals on large sheets of paper or a portable chalkboard. The trainer leads the critique or merely makes comments concerning the strengths and limitations of each plan. Three or four groups can be guided by one trainer through this variation.

Additional Materials

Davis and McCallum, *Planning, Conducting, and Evaluating Workshops,* Chapters 1–5
Knowles, *Modern Practice of Adult Education,* Chapter 8
Loughary and Hopson, *Producing Workshops, Seminars, and Short Courses,* Chapter 5
McKinley and Smith, *Guide to Program Planning*

For Censensus Decision-Making.   In collaborative learning, consensus constitutes a tentative working agreement that permits the group to move ahead with each person retaining a sense of responsibility for the decision. Nothing is more harmful to this kind of learning than quick and easy decisions that people have no stake in and few things are more valuable than being able to reach a consensus. The group may be deciding what is to be learned, why, how, when, or where; or it may be carrying out previous decisions, exploring a topic, assessing information, or practicing a skill. Each agreement will probably require people to make concessions, to give and take a bit. Although it is rare that everyone is totally pleased when a decision is made, the effects are superior to voting, a process through which nearly half the members may lose. Losing tends to have negative effect on most people's motivation to learn and to take responsibility for implementing decisions.

Training is usually directed toward increased skill in reconciling conflicting viewpoints, a positive attitude toward consensus decision-making, and the ability to verify when a valid consensus is reached.

When a decision has been reached, a valid consensus usually exists when the group members can go along with the decision ungrudgingly (if not necessarily ecstatically), have the feeling that a sincere effort was made to give each member an opportunity for input, feel that it is "their" decision, and stand ready to reexamine the decision as necessary (i.e., regard it as tentative).

Activities

1. For an ongoing group, assign one or more observers to a regularly scheduled meeting at which group decisions will be important (not a session, for example, that will be given over to listening to a speaker or learning from resource persons in some comparable manner). The observer is instructed to watch for and record information concerning how the group reaches decisions and evidence of the effects of those decisions.

After the observer's report, the trainer leads a critique built around these questions: What seems to constitute decision making for this group? What are some effects of the way decisions are reached? To what extent does consensus apparently take place? Can we achieve more valid and meaningful consensus? How?

Conclude with a brief presentation concerning what a consensus is, its potential effects on group task accomplishment and learning, and the individual actions that foster a consensus.

2. Establish leaderless groups of five or six members. Give each person a list of about eight items that are relevant for this audience—well-known objects, people, events, or occupations. Everyone receives the same list. Give the groups about fifteen minutes to rank the items on the list (e.g., "Which of the eight persons on the list has contributed the most to our profession?" or, "Which event had the greatest effect on our nation's historical development?"). Impose these rules: no voting, no horse trading, seek the best collective judgment, include everyone in the decision.

After the rankings are made, a critique can focus on how decisions were made, how group members feel about the decisions, and what might have contributed to a more valid consensus.

Variation:
Precede the group decision-making activity with a five-minute period during which individuals rank the items. Individuals may then later compare their own rankings with those of their group.

Additional Materials

Bergevin and McKinley, *Participation Training for Adult Education,* pp. 77–78, 101
McKinley, *Participants Manual,* pp. 11, 21–22
Pfeiffer and Jones, Vols. II and III

Training for Learning Through Educational Institutions

This kind of training aims to help people get the most from the programs and resources found in schools and colleges. As we saw in chapter 7, the concerns to be dealt with include students' rights, the criteria for assessing institutions' offerings and activities, using instructors as resources for learning, and study-skills improvement. Study-skills improvement will be emphasized here.

Training comes from two main sources. The first is individual instructors who accept responsibility for helping students to learn about learning; the second is the institution itself. Many colleges and universities make training available for studying, memorizing, note-taking, report writing, exam taking, and using libraries and learning centers. For example, Ohlone (Ohio) has developed a system that includes eight individualized courses, sixty-one videotapes, and a handbook (Maloney 1980). Well over half of the community colleges in the United States have specialists in remediation on the staff (Cross 1976).

Some institutions provide training that is oriented less to coping and more to such matters as the understanding of learning processes and of self as learner. Students in the weekend program at the College of Notre Dame (Baltimore, Maryland) receive credit for a seminar designed to help them to recognize their learning style and develop analytical and critical skills (*Chronicle of Higher Education,* November 17, 1975). Clark University (Worcester, Massachusetts) has experimented with comprehensive, broad-gauged training.

Carolyn Coulter, a former staff member at Clark, described in a letter to me a "Learning About Learning" course for returning students she conducted there for several years. The purposes and goals included to present and develop for the students an understanding of thinking processes, to help students understand and appreciate nonlinear and intuitive thinking and problem solving, and to help students to assume more authority for their own learning. The thirteen weekly class sessions combined lectures (on such topics as educational assumptions, learning style, and human development) with exercises (on reflection, attention, listening, consensus). Recommended reading included the writings of such developmentalists as Erik Erikson, Roger Gould, and Lawrence Kohlberg. The students were required to submit a series of short papers employing a three-part format: (1) a description of a personally important learning with the emphasis on the behavior and feelings of those involved; (2) an analysis of what happened (the situation) in terms of assumptions, with theory found in the course to be applied; and (3) an experiment to formulate a way of changing, to pose for oneself an alternative course of action ("If the same thing happened again, what would you do differently?").

New Perceptions of Training Needs of College Students

As with most in-depth training, the Clark course on "Learning About Learning" rested, correctly I believe, on the assumption that students (trainees) will most profit (learn to learn) from increasing the ability to look objectively at learning and their place in it (at their meanings, personal constructs, assumptions, and strategies).

Similar approaches are being developed abroad. In Sweden, Roger Säljo (1979) developed a method for helping people to become more aware of their learning processes and to stop equating learning with schooling. Säljo's method is based on written descriptions of how students go about studying and what learning means to them. Laurie Thomas and Sheila Harri-Augstein (1977), working in Britain, urge the tutor (instructor) and trainee to assume joint responsibility for bringing the student's personal learning processes under review by means of "learning conversations." The instructor and student learn how to clarify the purposes for learning and evaluative criteria from the needs of the learner. The trainee should gradually be helped to take over increasing amounts of the instructor's responsibilities. Thomas and Harri-Augstein report achieving such effects through training that uses a "repertory grid" as a basis for encouraging the student to "exhibit part of his system of personal constructs" and for eliciting learning conversations with others and with himself or herself.

Several other researchers are using the personal-construct theory originated by George Kelly (1955) and the repertory grid to develop training designs, exercises, and materials (Candy 1980; Entwistle and Hounsell 1975; Keen and Pope 1981).

The kind of training described above by Coulter, Säljo, and Thomas and Harri-Augstein arises in part from dissatisfaction with the so-called cookbook methods for students to acquire what other people judge to be good study habits (i.e., the typical how-to-study manual and training activity). Graham Gibbs's (1981) important work *Teaching Students to Learn* derives from a similar orientation. Like the others, Gibbs advocates a "learner-centered" approach. Noting the existence of more than 100 how-to-study manuals in English, he asks why such books usually don't do the trick. He cites several reasons. First of all, merely "telling" (as a training procedure) doesn't usually change behavior when deep-rooted, habitual ways of doing things are involved. Secondly, we don't know for sure what the necessary study skills consist of. Research is inadequate, with contradictory findings. Thirdly, successful students have developed personal strategies that may not work for others. The sophisticated and the inept learner may be almost indistinguishable in terms of observable study habits. Finally, appropriate learning and study techniques can be presumed to vary with the subject matter and the course goals.

The implications are not that how-to-study resources and training efforts are useless but rather that nonspecific training in a vacuum stands to accomplish little: "If we give advice in a *generalized* way, without regard to the individual student, or the particular course he is taking (or the demands of its assessment system), then it won't be very likely that we'll have a positive effect" (Gibbs 1981, p. 97f). Graham Gibbs has found students' reflections about their studying to be the cornerstone of study-skills development and states that the reconceptualizing of a study task will often bring about significant change (Gibbs 1981, p. 97). Effective training requires that the instructor (or counselor) and student look carefully at the characteristics of the subject matter to be learned, the institution's expectations, and some critical learning tasks involved. The student needs to become aware of the influence of context and its implications for what and how he or she should learn. The training works best when instructors can at least temporarily de-emphasize their authority role.

Gibbs builds his approach around six training exercises (Learning, Reading, Taking Notes, Writing, Taking Exams, Organizing Yourself), a rationale for their use, and suggestions for implementing them. The work constitutes an excellent guide to training for improved learning in courses and classes. It is well grounded in experience and in research involving a wide variety of classes and students. The distinction between training and instruction is clearly and consistently made, and the educational milieu for this kind of learning is realistically taken into account. The following section owes much to Gibbs.

Activities and Exercises for Learning Through Educational Institutions

For Legitimizing Training and Getting Commitment to Change. This kind of training is most often conducted at the outset of a multipurpose training activity or early in a course in which the instructor intends to combine training with instruction in subject matter. It aims at creating awareness, establishing a diagnostic frame of mind, and fostering trainee interest in learning about processes.

Activities

1. Conduct the Thinking About Learning Exercise (Appendix D), or a personal adaptation of it, as an introduction to and foundation for more specific training. (Takes about one and a half hours.)

2. Have trainees (working alone) develop a list of their three greatest strengths and three greatest weaknesses as students. Then have them meet in pairs to compare and contrast the items on the lists and share reactions. (Allow ten minutes.) Now ask each person to reflect silently on what has

transpired and write a statement of one specific improvement in study skills he or she would be willing to invest time and energy in trying to bring about (e.g., to work out a better system of keeping track of written sources used in preparing research papers). The statement should be signed. (Allow five minutes.)

Collect the statements and schedule private conferences with each person to verify the need for and strength of commitment to the desired change; agree on the remedial activity to be undertaken.

Schedule a follow-up meeting to discuss results.

For Improved Reading.   Training usually aims at helping people to become more conscious of their assumptions about reading and their reading habits. Reading with increased flexibility is often a goal. When an instructor trains his or her own students, activity may focus on the reading requirements of the kinds of materials found in the particular subject area and on the specific texts or other materials (e.g., novels or technical reports) to be read for the course.

Activities

1. Introduce the subject of reading improvement briefly and then have trainees work through the Active Reading Exercise (Appendix B). Lead a discussion designed to draw out specific implications for the subject matter and required reading for the course in question.

2. Demonstrate for about five minutes how to "attack" a book by examining a course text and talking aloud to yourself as it is done. How much does it weigh? When was it published? How is it organized? What does the table of contents tell me? Does it have an index? special features? What does the author say or imply about the purpose of the book and getting the most from it? How am I going to use the book for the purposes of this course's goals and assignments? Invite comment on what was done and how students themselves might prefer to approach a book.

3. Conclude an occasional class session with a brief period of discussion initiated by a question such as, Are there particular problems you're having with the text? Offer, and invite students to offer, tentative solutions to the problems identified (e.g., a source of definitions for some of the basic terms the author seems to take for granted).

Additional Materials

Gibbs, *Teaching Students to Learn, pp.* 24–33
Hamblin, *Teaching Study Skills,* pp. 43–56
Houle, *Continuing Your Education,* Chapter 6

For Improved Note-taking.   Note-taking serves different purposes; often the maintaining of attention during a lecture, or while reading, is the main one. Training can make students aware of the purpose of their note-taking in different situations and the need to put their notes in a form that later makes possible a differentiated use such as for preparing to write exams, for class discussion, or for the writing of reports or research papers. The best system for taking notes is one that is most useful to the individual in a specific setting.

Activities

1. Give a ten-minute lecture or ask a colleague to give one while the trainees take notes in their normal manner. They then work in pairs to compare and contrast what they found important and the form they use in recording information (e.g., great detail, main ideas, tag words).

   Consider having each person explain to the total group the advantages and disadvantages of his or her partner's approach to note-taking. Discuss possible adjustments in strategies.

   Variations:

   Have the trainee do the same with a set of notes from a
       previous lecture.
   Videotape the lecture so that people can see it a second time
       and make judgments about the adequacy of their notes.

2. Give a lecture (or present a recorded one) and have the trainees use Apps's note-taking system (1978, p. 32) for taking notes.

   Lead a period of analysis concerning how people feel about using someone else's note-taking system. Who found it useful? Why? What modifications would individuals wish to make before adopting it?

Additional Materials

Apps, *Study Skills,* Chapter 2
Gibbs, *Teaching Students to Learn,* pp. 18–23
Houle, *Continuing Your Education,* Chapter 5

For Coping with Exams.   As with reading and note-taking, people have developed characteristic ways of preparing for exams and for conducting themselves during the exam itself. Some of these mechanisms and habits are likely to hinder, while others are not. Training can deal with preparation strategies, with tactics for use during the exam, or with both. Training of the first type focuses on helping people learn how to think clearly about the nature and purpose of an exam, encouraging them to read and take notes with course goals and the purposes of particular exams or quizzes in mind, and fostering an understanding of the difference between knowing and demonstrating what you know (and the implications of this).

Activity related to exam sitting usually aims at helping students cope with anxiety, utilize their time more efficiently, and avoid such common blunders as misreading or misunderstanding questions. When the course instructor trains the students, the overall evaluation system for the course can be reviewed and people can be helped to understand and deal with the particular types of tests expected to be used. This requires the instructor to examine and reveal personal assumptions about evaluation and how it should be done. Some soul-searching may be involved; training will probably be ineffective if the instructor does not genuinely desire all students to attain high ratings.

Activities

1. Distribute copies of a "good" and a "poor" student examination paper. Help trainees to identify the strengths of one and the limitations of the other.

2. Have groups of three to six persons discuss for about ten minutes the question, "What causes me anxiety in testing situations?" List some of the recurring items mentioned on the chalkboard. Assign one item to each group and ask the members to develop suggestions for coping with or minimizing the anxiety involved. Provide consultation later for individuals who want to explore the matter further.

3. These three activities are for improvement in the taking of major comprehensive exams.

   a. Ask people to go outside the room and enter as if they were coming in to sit for a major exam. Give them the directions for taking an exam in a *nonsupportive* way in order to simulate a threatening introduction to an experience already envisioned by them as a threatening one. After the exam instructions and getting under way have been simulated, lead a period of analysis by asking questions like these: How did you feel? Was it anxiety producing? Why? What will you do if this kind of exam reception comes your way? How will you cope with it?

b. Have trainees fill out the Test Anxiety Checklist (Appendix G). Conduct a general analysis of the results or have people meet in groups of two or three to share and discuss their concerns.

Variation:

Precede the use of the checklist and critique with a short impromptu test (in mathematics, for example).

c. Demonstrate, or have demonstrated, one or two relaxation techniques of potential value during exams.

4. This activity gives better results with essay questions. Prepare copies of an essay question on a topic about which the trainees can be presumed to be somewhat knowledgeable. Ask them to try to answer the question just as they would under actual examination conditions.

After five or ten minutes, have them stop writing and work in two- or three-person groups to compare and contrast how they went about using their allotted time. Ask one person from each group to sum up differences and similarities in approaches.

Lead the total group in a discussion of the following questions and others that arise: What are the most useful things to do in the first few minutes? What should be avoided? *Variation.* Repeat the first phase once (with a different question) before leading the critique involving the total group.

Additional Materials

Apps, *Study Skills,* Chapter 2
Gibbs, *Teaching Students to Learn,* pp. 42–44
Houle, *Continuing Your Education,* Chapter 9
Chapter 7

Instructors as Trainers

Subject-matter specialists who train the students in their courses will need to make special efforts to avoid certain problems they most likely will encounter. An ingrained orientation toward the discipline that is their life's work may inhibit the ability to think clearly about learning and about learners, thereby working against sound training design and accurate diagnosis of learning problems. The authority that goes with the instructor's role may tend to hinder establishment of the mutual trust that fosters student self-examination and leads to change in learning-related behavior. It is also natural for instructors to hesitate to cut into classroom time for training activity. And some instructors may find it awkward to move back and forth from content to process.

In seeking to minimize the difficulties that go with the territory, instructors will need to think carefully about the environment for training. Moving the class to another setting—to a room in a learning center or a lounge, for example—can prove useful. Transitions are also important. A short break, perhaps accompanied by some rearranging of furniture, may aid the instructor in switching from teacher to trainer role and the class members in switching from student to trainee roles.

The instructor may find it useful to cooperate with a colleague. Collaboration in the planning and conducting of training has several potential advantages as long as a good fit obtains. Cotrainers can monitor each other for dysfunctional behavior. They may stimulate each other's thinking in the direction of innovative design and adaptation of already existing exercises. And the instructor from down the hall will probably be vested with the special authority normally accorded the visiting expert.

The instructor who accepts responsiblity for providing training that helps students learn how to learn more effectively usually faces no easy task. It is a responsibility of a high order, one with much potential for rewards for both teacher and student. Together they will need to feel their way and to take some risks. Eventually both will be able to share in the satisfactions that their persistence will almost surely bring.

Appendixes A-J

APPENDIX A.   Some Learning-Style Inventories

Cognitive Aspects of Learning Style

Name of Inventory	What It Assesses	Format	Sources of Further Information
Embedded Figures Test	Field-dependence/ independence (perceiving and getting meaning)	A booklet with twenty-five designs hidden in the marble	Consulting Psychologists Press, 577 College Avenue, Palo Alto, CA 94306
Kolb's Learning Styles Inventory	How an individual adapts or learns from experience	Rank ordering the words in nine four-word sets	McBer and Company, 136 Newberry Street, Boston, MA 02116
Conceptual Styles Test	Analytical versus relational (thinking and grouping things)	Select two pictures from sets of three	Goldstein and Blackman 1978
Matching Familiar Figures Test	Reflectivity versus impulsivity	Pictures of sets of objects only one of which is identical to the standard	Krumboltz 1965, pp. 133–61; NASSP 1979
Transaction Ability Inventory	"Your Natural Means of Transacting with Your Environments"	Rank ordering the words in ten four-word sets describing oneself (e.g., intake information "randomly" or "sequentially")	Gregorc 1979
Your Style of Learning and Thinking—Form C	Tendency to emphasize left or right side of the brain (or mixed) when thinking and learning	Forty-item forced-choice questionnaire	Department of Educational Psychology, University of Georgia, Athens, GA 30601

Broad-gauged Inventories

Name of Inventory	What It Assesses	Format	Sources of Further Information
Canfield Learning Styles Inventory (CLS)	Preferences for structure, environment, climate, sensory modalities, expectations	Forced ranking of four choices in thirty questions	Humanics Media, Liberty Drawer 7970, Ann Arbor, MI 48107
Productivity Environmental Preference Survey (PEPS) (children's version available)	How adults prefer to function, learn, concentrate, and perform in occupational or educational tasks	Reaction to one hundred items on a Likert-type scale	Price Systems, Box 3271, Lawrence, KS 66044
Grasha-Riechmann Student Learning Styles Questionnaire	Preferred styles: competitive, collaborative, avoidant, participant, dependent, independent	Reaction to ninety items on a Likert-type scale	Faculty Resource Center, University of Cincinnati, Cincinnati, OH 45221
Excursion Styles Inventory	Tendency to learn and enter into things with imagination/ enthusiasm or logic/ practicality	Self-rating on twenty-eight pairs of opposing words	Hagberg and Leider 1978

Miscellaneous Inventories

Name of Inventory	What it Assesses	Format	Sources of Further Information
Self-Directed Learning Readiness Scale	Extent of capability for exercising autonomy when learning	Self-report questionnaire with fifty-eight Likert-type items	Guglielmino and Associates, 734 Marble Way, Boca Raton, FL 33432
Myers-Briggs Type Indicator	Preferences for thinking, feeling, perceiving, intuiting, sensing, judging together with extroversion versus introversion	Forced-choice questionnaire with 166 items	Consulting Psychologists Press, 577 College Avenue, Palo Alto, CA 94306
Learning Preference Inventory (Adult Basic Education)	Student preferences when learning tasks, skills, and knowledge	Pictures of learning situations and a set of related questions	Manzo 1975
FIRO-B	Three characteristics of interpersonal relations—behavior expressed toward, and wanted from, others—inclusion, control, affection	Forced-choice questionnaire with fifty-four items	Consulting Psychologists Press, 577 College Avenue, Palo Alto, CA 94306
Learning Activities Opinionnaire (Vocational Education)	Preferences for concrete versus symbolic and structured versus unstructured instruction	Self-assessment on twenty-two Likert-type items	Oen 1973
Life Styles Inventory	Twelve basic styles of behavior toward the world	Self-assessment through forced choice	Human Synergistics, 39819 Plymouth Road, Plymouth, MI 48170
Adaptive Style Inventory	The way one characteristically adapts to different situations—toward concrete experience or reflective observation, abstract conceptualization or active experimentation	Self-description test with eight items; six sets of paired statements requiring a choice to go with each item	McBer and Company, 136 Newberry Street, Boston, MA 02116

APPENDIX B.   Active Reading Exercise

You will need writing material and a nonfiction book that you are not familiar with. The book should have a dust jacket, a table of contents, some front matter (foreword, preface, introduction) and an index.

1. Turn to the inside front of the dust jacket and read what the publisher has to say about the book.

2. Turn to the back of the dust jacket and read what the publisher has to say about the author and his or her qualifications to write such a book.

3. Turn to the front matter (foreword, preface, introduction) and read the author's or editor's orientation to the book.

4. Turn to the table of contents and see how the author has organized the information into parts, chapters, or other subsections.

5. Leaf through the book rapidly scanning or reading the occasional paragraph or heading that interests you. Try to get the feel of the book.

6. Put the book down and write three questions concerning matters you have become curious about as a result of this preliminary examination.

7. Next, review your first question and find in it a key word or phrase that you think might be in the index. Go to the index and look for the key word; if you draw a blank, try to come up with a synonym. If the synonym isn't there, see if the table of contents leads you to where the question can be answered.

8. Now turn to that part of the book that deals with your question and look for the answer. If the author refers to material in other parts of the book, follow the leads until you have enough information relevant to your question.

9. Use the same procedure with your second and third questions.

Questions

1. How differently did you feel about using a book as a resource for learning from the way you usually feel about a book?

2. Is there any difference in the quality of the information you have gained?

APPENDIX C. Requesting Feedback Exercise

With the whole group seated in a circle (a large group can be divided into subgroups of at least five persons), let anyone who wishes to seek information from those present ask questions about the way other group members have seen his or her behavior. For example, a group member might say (referring to the list below) "I would like to know how you see me in relation to number 8." If any person can give specific information concerning what has been asked for, he or she will contribute to the other group member's self-appraisal.

To use this method successfully, three rules should be followed.

Participation is voluntary. No member shall be compelled either to seek or to give information.

The information given shall be limited to what a person asks for.

Observations should be substantiated by facts, by specifics of what has been said or done.

1. Expresses self clearly and concisely.
2. Encourages group to keep at the job.
3. Takes the lead in initiating topics, concerns, and procedures.
4. Offers constructive ideas as needed.
5. Contributes without cutting others off.
6. Helps get to the meat of issues.
7. Listens attentively to what others say.
8. Helps others express their ideas and learn.
9. Helps others feel at ease and is supportive.
10. Sticks too long to his or her point.
11. Avoids facing problems.
12. Seeks to impose his or her will on the group.
13. Occasionally gets defensive.

APPENDIX **D.   Thinking About Learning Exercise**

Objectives

To see what assumptions about learning the training-group members have brought with them

To establish a diagnostic frame of reference for learning about learning

Resources

Chalkboard or easel
Paper and pencil for each person

Time Required

One to one and a half hours

Procedure

1. Introduce the exercise as you see fit.

2. Ask the trainees to think back to a particularly bad learning experience—one found to be boring, frightening, wasteful, or somehow unpleasant. Ask them to jot down a few notes (phrases and tag words) about why it was a bad learning experience. (Allow 3 minutes.)

3. Ask the trainees to repeat the same procedure for a particularly good learning experience they recall—one where they were successful or learned a lot. (Allow 3 minutes.)

4. Have the trainees pair up. Then give them these instructions:

   a. Share your experiences and your interpretations of why they are good or bad.

   b. What are some similarities and differences?

   c. What makes for good learning for both persons? for bad learning for both persons?

   d. Try to stay with personal experience. (Allow 10–15 minutes.)

5. Form groups of four by combining pairs.

   Instructions

   a. Pool your experience thus far to search for themes. What characterizes good and bad learning?

   b. Please have a recorder note some of your conclusions under two columns:

   What Leads to Unsatisfactory Learning?
   What Leads to Satisfactory Learning? (Allow 15 minutes.)

6. Dissolve the groups of four.

Instructions

a. Have each recorder in turn read to the total group one item from his or her group's list.

b. Record the items in two columns on the easel or chalkboard.

c. Encourage all trainees to ask for clarification of items as needed. (Continue as long as productive.)

d. The trainer now relates what has emerged to objectives of the exercise itself and his or her overall training goals.

Trainer Tips

Adapt the exercise to the group. Preplan for differences in group size, overall training purposes, and previous formal training of group members in learning theory. Take physical arrangements into account.

Establish an informal, nonthreatening climate—there are no "right" answers.

Try to keep all activity focused on experience.

Think carefully about where the group will be when the exercise ends, the meaning of it for the trainee, and successfully bridging to the next phase of training.

Alternative

Begin with individual reflection on "How I Learn Best." Then proceed, through pairs and groups of four, to produce a list of themes.

APPENDIX E. **Learning from a Resource Person Exercise**

Objectives

To increase skill in gaining knowledge in a one-to-one learning situation

To encourage trainees to see other individuals as potential resources for learning

Resources

Chalkboard or easel
Multiple copies of "Guidelines" (see page 177)

Time Required

About one hour

Procedure

1. Prior to the session you have identified an area that you know something about that is not directly related to the subject of training. It may be a skill (e.g., scuba diving, chess, backpacking) or a knowledge area (local history, theology, butterflies, antique cars).

2. After introducing the exercise, explain to the group that you want a volunteer who is *not* knowledgeable in the subject to interview you briefly in order for him or her to learn more about it.

3. Having gotten the volunteer interviewer, ask group members to suggest some questions that the interviewer can put to you. Ask the interviewer to jot down a few. (Allow 3 minutes.)

4. The interview is conducted before the group; the interviewer seeks to get useful information related to the questions the group members have identified and to any that he or she improvises.

   Instructions

   a. Ask the group to observe the interaction of the interview carefully and to refrain from verbal comments while it is carried out.

   b. Encourage the interviewer in advance to do whatever he or she can to facilitate communication and personal understanding of the subject while the interview is conducted.

5. During the interview respond to the interviewer's questions in such ways as to inhibit communication (use jargon, overly technical language, fuzzy explanations, etc.). Exhibit little effort to find out how you can be most helpful to the interviewer. (Allow 5 minutes.)

6. After closing out the interview, ask the interviewer how he or she felt in the role and what he or she did to try to learn and to cope with the problems that emerged. (Allow 3 minutes.)

7. Have the trainees pair off. Ask each pair to share ideas about how the interviewer might have better prepared for the interview if there had been time to do so. (Allow 5 minutes.)

8. Ask the trainee pairs to conduct (simultaneously) interviews on their own after one has agreed to interview the other concerning a subject he or she is knowledgeable about, and they've planned together concerning how the resource person might be most useful to the interviewer and identified some possible obstacles to communication and understanding. (Allow about 15 minutes, 10 for planning and 5 for conducting the interviews.)

9. Close out the interviews and ask the trainee pairs to discuss with each other how their plans worked out. (Allow 3–5 minutes.)

10. Dissolve the trainee pairs and ask all group members to join you in developing a list on the chalkboard or easel of some guidelines for planning.

11. Pass out the "Guidelines" sheet (see page 177) and compare it with the guidelines you have listed on the chalkboard or easel.

Trainer Tips

Try to ensure that the initial interview of you does not lapse into slapstick.

Keep in mind (and in the trainees' minds) that the skills involved concern using another person as a resource for *learning*.

Alternative

A second trainer occasionally interrupts the interview to call attention to key process factors. If a second trainer is present, the interview may be role-played by trainers. This usually makes for a more certain relevance to the training objectives; however, less trainee involvement usually transpires.

Guidelines for Learning from a Resource Person

Planning

1. Clarify what you want to learn. Write it down.
2. Anticipate communication problems.
3. Consider the environmental factors.
4. Put yourself in the resource person's place. What's in it for him or her?
5. Orient the resource person ahead of time.

During the Meeting

1. Try to make your interests and objectives clear: "I want to learn enough of the technical vocabulary of investing to understand the advice of professional advisers and brokers." "I'd like to be able to play well enough to enjoy the game by the end of the summer."
2. Be moderately assertive: "I'm afraid I don't follow that." "Could you give an example?" "Would you show me again more slowly?" "May I try it now?" "May I try to summarize?"
3. Give and seek feedback: "That's very helpful." "Am I asking the right questions?" "What do you think I ought to do next?" "I'm further along than I expected to be." "To be honest, that's more than I care to know about penguins."

APPENDIX **F.   A Learning Contract Form**

Learner _____   Learning Project or Topic _____

Learning Objectives	Learning Resources and Strategies	Target Date for Completion	Evidence of Accomplishment of Objectives

APPENDIX G.   Test Anxiety Checklist

Can you identify with any of these common thoughts and worries that people with test anxiety have? Check those that you can identify with the most.

1. Worry About Performance

___ I should have reviewed more. I'll never get through.

___ My mind is a blank. I'll never get the answer. I must really be stupid.

___ I can't remember a thing. This always happens to me.

___ Only ten minutes left. There are so many questions. I'll never get through everything.

___ It's no use. I might as well give up.

___ I knew this stuff yesterday. What is wrong with me?

___ I have to get a high score.

___ This stuff is easy, so I should get everything right.

___ This is terrible. This is absolutely the worst test I've ever taken.

2. Worry About Bodily Reactions

___ I'm sick. I'll never get through.

___ I'm sweating all over—it's really hot in here.

___ My hands are shaking again. I can't even hold the lousy pen.

___ My stomach is going crazy, churning and jumping all over.

___ Here it comes—I'm getting really tense again. Normal people just don't get like this.

3. Worry About How Others Are Doing

___ I know everyone's doing better than I am.

___ I must be the dumbest one in the group.

___ I am going to be the last one done again. I must really be stupid.

___ No one else seems to be having trouble. Am I the only one?

4. Worry About Possible Negative Consequences

___ If I fail this test, I'll never get into the program.

___ I'll never graduate.

___ I'll think less of myself.

___ I'll be embarrassed.

___ Everyone will be disappointed in me.

APPENDIX H.   Procedures, Strategies, and Desired Outcomes

Type of Desired Outcome	Most Appropriate Procedure or Strategy
Knowledge (Generalizations about experience; internalization of information)	Lecture, television, debate, dialogue, interview, symposium, panel, group interview, colloquy, motion picture, slide film, recording, book-based discussion, reading
Understanding (Application of information and generalizations)	Audience participation, demonstration, motion picture, dramatization, Socratic dialogue, problem-solving discussion, case discussion, critical-incident process, case method, games
Skills (Incorporation of new ways of performing through practice)	Role playing, in-basket exercises, games, action mazes, participative cases, T-group, nonverbal exercises, skill practice exercises, drill, coaching
Attitudes (Adoption of new feelings through experiencing greater success with them than with old feelings)	Experience-sharing discussion, group-centered discussion, role playing, critical incident process, case method, games, participative cases, T-group, nonverbal exercises
Values (The adoption and priority arrangement of beliefs)	Television, lecture (sermon), debate, dialogue, symposium, colloquy, motion picture, dramatization, guided discussion, experience-sharing discussion, role playing, critical incident process, games, T-group
Interests (Satisfying exposure to new activities)	Television, demonstration, motion picture, slide film, dramatization, experience-sharing discussion, exhibits, trips, nonverbal exercises

APPENDIX I. Adult Teaching-Style Inventories

Name of Inventory	What It Assesses	Format	Sources of Further Information
Educational Orientation Questionnaire (EOQ)	Pedagogical versus andragogical orientation	Reaction to sixty statements with Likert-type scale	Hadley 1975
Principles of Adult Learning Scale (PALS)	Degree one accepts and tries to implement philosophy of prominent adult education theorists	Reaction to forty-four items on Likert-type scale	Conti 1979
Training Style Inventory (TSI)	Orientation toward four major theoretical areas: behaviorist, structuralist, functionist, humanist	Selecting one of four completion items for each of fifteen stem phrases	Brostrom 1979 Richard Brostrom COMCOR 6213 S. Highland Ave. Madison, WI 53705
Canfield Instructual Styles Inventory (CIS)	Preferences for different conditions and instructual techniques	Twenty-five forced-rank questions	Humanics Media, Liberty Drawer 7970 Ann Arbor, MI 48107

APPENDIX **J.   Collaborative Learning Appraisal Form**

	Agree	Disagree	Not Sure
1. The interest or need identified was an appropriate one	_____	_____	_____
2. Topics and goals were			
appropriate choices	_____	_____	_____
clearly focused	_____	_____	_____
well stated	_____	_____	_____
3. Evaluation was adequately provided for	_____	_____	_____
4. Resources, procedures, and strategies were			
appropriate choices	_____	_____	_____
adapted to learners' characteristics	_____	_____	_____
carried out effectively	_____	_____	_____
5. The time schedule was realistic	_____	_____	_____
6. The physical arrangements were satisfactory	_____	_____	_____

7. What might have contributed to a more effective planning effort?

8. As the program was conducted, what might have been done differently to foster learning by those involved?

Bibliography

Alinsky, Saul D. *Rules for Radicals*. New York: Random House, 1972.

Apps, Jerold W. *Study Skills for Those Adults Returning to School*. New York: McGraw-Hill, 1978.

————.*The Adult Learner on Campus*. Chicago: Follett Publishing Company, 1981.

————. *Improving Your Writing Skills: A Learning Plan for Adults*. Chicago: Follett Publishing Company, 1982.

Aslanian, Carol, and Brickell, Henry M. *Americans in Transition: Life Changes as Reasons for Adult Learning*. Princeton, N.J.: College Entrance Examination Board, 1980.

Ausubel, David P. *Educational Psychology: A Cognitive View*. New York: Holt, Rinehart, and Winston, 1968.

Benne, Kenneth, et al. *The Laboratory Method of Changing and Learning*. Palo Alto, Calif.: Science and Behavior Books, 1975.

Bergevin, Paul E. *A Philosophy for Adult Education*. New York: Seabury Press, 1967.

Bergevin, Paul E., and McKinley, John. *Participation Training for Adult Education*. St. Louis, Mo.: The Bethany Press, 1967.

————. *Adult Education for the Church*. St. Louis, Mo.: The Bethany Press, 1971.

Bergevin, Paul E.; McKinley, John; and Smith, Robert M. "The Adult Education Activity: Content, Processes, and Procedures." In *Adult Education: Outlines of an Emerging Field of University Study*, edited by Gale Jensen et al., pp. 270–89. Washington, D.C.: Adult Education Association of the U.S.A., 1964.

Bergevin, Paul E.; Morris, Dwight; and Smith, Robert M. *Adult Education Procedures.* Greenwich, Conn.: Seabury Press, 1963.

Berquist, William H., and Phillips, Steven R. *A Handbook for Faculty Development.* Washington, D.C.: The Council for the Advancement of Small Colleges, 1975.

Billings, Karen, and Moursund, David. *Are You Computer Literate?* Portland, Oreg.: Dilithium, 1979.

Blaney, Jack. "Program Development and Curricular Authority." In *Program Development and Education,* edited by Jack Blaney et al. Vancouver, B.C.: University of British Columbia, Center for Continuing Education, 1974, pp. 2–25.

Bolles, Richard N. *The Three Boxes of Life.* Berkeley, Calif.: Ten Speed Press, 1978.

Bolton, Elizabeth B. "A Conceptual Analysis of the Mentor Relationship in the Career Development of Women." *Adult Education* 30(1980): 195–207.

Botkin, James W., et al. *No Limits to Learning.* Oxford: Pergamon, 1979.

Bowren, Fay F., and Zintz, Miles V. *Teaching Reading in Adult Basic Education.* Dubuque, Iowa: William C. Brown, 1977.

Bradford, Leland P., et al. eds. *T-Group Theory and Laboratory Method.* New York: John Wiley, 1964.

Brittain, Vera Mary. *Testament of Youth.* New York: Seaview Books, 1980.

Brostrom, Richard. "Training Style Inventory (TSI)." In *The 1979 Annual Handbook for Group Facilitators,* edited by J. William Pfeiffer and John E. Jones, LaJolla. Calif.: University Associates, 1979.

Brown, Ann L., et al. "Learning to Learn: On Training Students to Learn from Texts." *Educational Researcher,* February 1981, pp. 14–21.

Brundage, D. H., and MacKeracher, D. *Adult Learning Principles and Their Application to Program Planning.* Toronto: Ministry of Education, Ontario, 1980.

Bruner, Jerome S. *The Process of Education.* New York: Vintage, 1963.

Buckley, Elizabeth. "Pilot Project in Computer Assisted Instruction." Great Neck, N.Y.: Adult Learning Centers, 1979.

Candy, P. C. *A Personal Construct Approach to Adult Learning.* Underdale, South Australia: Adelaide College of the Arts and Education, 1980.

Castaneda, Carlos. *The Teachings of Don Juan: A Yaqui Way of Knowledge.* New York: Ballantine, 1968.

Christie, Richard, and Jahoda, Marie. *The Authoritarian Personality.* Glencoe, Ill.: The Free Press, 1954.

Clark, Frances. "Fantasy and Imagination." In *Four Psychologies Applied to Education,* edited by Thomas B. Roberts. pp. 498–513. New York: John Wiley, 1975.

Claxton, C. S., and Ralston, Y. *Learning Styles: Their Impact on Teaching and Administration.* AAHE-ERIC Higher Education Research Report, no. 10. Washington, D.C.: American Association for Higher Education, 1978.

Conti, Gary J. "Principles of Adult Learning Scale." Proceedings of the Twentieth Adult Education Research Conterence, April 1979, Ann Arbor, Michigan, pp. 64–70.

Cronbach, Lee J., and Snow, Richard E. *Aptitudes and Instructional Methods.* New York: John Wiley, 1977.

Cross, K. Patricia. *Accent on Learning.* San Francisco: Jossey-Bass, 1976.

————. *The Missing Link: Connecting Adult Learning to Learning Resources.* New York: College Entrance Examination Board, 1978.

Curran, Charles A. *Counseling Learning: A Whole Person Model for Education.* Apple River, Ill.: Apple River Press, 1977.

Dale, Edgar. *Building a Learning Environment.* Bloomington, Ind.: Phi Delta Kappa, 1972.

————. *The Good Mind.* Bloomington, Ind.: Phi Delta Kappa, 1978.

Daly, Brian E. "Attacking That Aging Feeling: Learning and Aging," 1976, ED 173 672.

Davis, Larry N., and McCallon, Earl. *Planning, Conducting, and Evaluating Workshops.* Austin, Tex.: Learning Concepts, 1975.

Day, H. I., et al. *Intrinsic Motivation.* Toronto: Holt, Rinehart, and Winston, 1971.

Della-Dora, Delmo, and Blanchard, Jerry, eds. *Moving Toward Self-Directed Learning.* Washington, D.C.: Association for Supervision and Curriculum Development, 1979.

Denis, Margaret. "Intuitive Learning Among Adults." Unpublished doctoral dissertation, University of Toronto, 1975.

"The Design of Self-Directed Learning: A Program of Videotapes and Written Materials." Toronto: Ontario Institute for Studies in Education, 1981.

Dewey, John. *Democracy and Education.* New York: Free Press, 1966.

Dickinson, Leslie, and Carver, David. "Learning How to Learn: Steps Toward Self-Direction in Foreign Language Learning in Schools." *English Language Teaching* 35(1980): 1–7.

Donnarumma, Theresa, et al. "Success in a High School Completion Program and Its Relation to Field Dependence-Independence." *Adult Education* 30(1980): 222–32.

Draves, Bill. *The Free University: A Model for Lifelong Learning.* Chicago: Follett Publishing Company, 1980.

Dunn, Rita. "Learning: A Matter of Style." A videotape and a discussion guide. Alexandria, Va.: Association for Supervision and Curriculum Development, 1979.

Dunn, Rita, and Dunn, Kenneth. *Administrator's Guide to New Programs for Faculty Management and Evaluation.* West Nyack, N.Y.: Parker Publishing Company, 1977.

Dunn, Rita, and Price, Gary. *Teaching Students Through Their Individual Learning Styles.* Reston, Va.: Reston Publishing Company, 1978.

Durrell, Lawrence. *Mountolive.* New York: Dutton, 1959.

Elliott, Paul H. *An Exploratory Study of Adult Learning Styles.* Washington, D.C.: The Model School for the Deaf, Kendall Green, 1976.

Entwistle, N., and Hounsell, D. *How Students Learn.* Lancaster, England: Institute for Research and Development in Post Compulsory Education, 1975.

Fales, Ann, and Greey, Mary. "The Puzzle of Mid-Life Learning: What Are the Pieces?" *Yearbook of Adult and Continuing Education.* Chicago: Marquis Academic Media, 1980–81.

Faure, Edgar, et al. eds. *Learning to Be.* Paris: UNESCO, 1972.

Ferguson, Marilyn. *The Acquarian Conspiracy: Personal and Social Transformation in the 1980s.* Los Angeles: J. P. Tarcher, 1980.

Feringer, Richard. "Problems of Teaching the Indigent." *Continuing Higher Education* (Pennsylvania State University) vol. 27, no. 4 (Fall 1979).

Fischer, Barbara B., and Fischer, Louis. "Styles in Teaching and Learning." *Educational Leadership* 36(1979): 245–54.

Freedman, Richard D., and Stumpf, Stephen A. "Learning Style Theory: Less Than Meets the Eye." *Academy of Management Review* 5(1980): 445–47.

Freire, Paulo. *The Pedagogy of the Oppressed.* New York: Seabury Press, 1974.

Gibbs, Graham. *Teaching Students to Learn.* Milton Keynes, England: The Open University Press, 1981.

Gibbs, Graham, et al. "Understanding Why Students Don't Learn."
Study Methods Group Report, no. 5. Milton Keynes, England:
The Open University Press.

"Going to College Part-Time: What Catalogues, Bulletins, and
Programs Will Not Tell You." Chestnut Hill, Mass.: Boston
College Evening College, 1980.

Goldstein, K. M., and Blackman, Sheldon. *Cognitive Style*. New
York: John Wiley, 1978.

Grattan, C. Hartley, ed. *American Ideas About Adult Education*.
New York: Columbia University Press, 1959.

Gregorc, Anthony F. "Learning-Teaching Styles: Potent Forces
Behind Them." *Educational Leadership* 36(1979): 234–36.

Griffin, Virginia. "Self-Directed Adult Learners and Learning."
Learning 2(1979), no. 1:6–8, no. 2:12–15.

Gross, Ronald. *The Lifelong Learner*. New York: Simon and
Schuster, 1977.

Grover, David E. "A Study of Mediational Processes and Learning
to Learn." Doctoral dissertation, University of Kentucky, 1969.

Hadley, Herschal. "Development of an Instrument to Determine
Adult Educators' Orientation: Andragogical or Pedagogical."
Unpublished doctoral dissertation, Boston University, 1975.

Hagberg, J. O., and Leider, R. J. *The Inventurers: Excursions in Life
and Career Renewal.* Reading, Mass.: Addison-Wesley, 1978.

Haltsch, D. F. "Learning to Learn in Adulthood." *Journal of
Gerontology* 29(1974): 302–08.

Hamblin, Douglas H. *Teaching Study Skills*. Oxford: Basil Blackwell,
1981.

Hamkins, George. "Motivation and Individual Learning Styles."
Engineering Education 64(1974): 408–11.

Hart, Joseph K. *Light From the North*. New York: Henry Holt,
1926.

Havighurst, Robert J. *Developmental Tasks and Education*. New
York: David McKay, 1972.

Hill, Joseph E. *The Educational Sciences: A Conceptual Framework*.
West Bloomfield, Mich.: Hill Educational Sciences Foundation,
1981.

Hortin, John A. "Visual Literacy—The Theoretical Foundations."
Unpublished doctoral dissertation, Northern Illinois University,
1980.

Houle, Cyril O. *Continuing Your Education*. New York: McGraw-
Hill, 1964.

————. *Continuing Learning in the Professions*. San Francisco: Jossey-Bass, 1980.

Humphrey, F. Charles. "A Study of Adults' Preferences for Control of Molar Learning Activities." Paper read at the Adult Education Research Conference, April 1974, in Chicago, Ill., ED 094 103.

Hunt, David E., et al. *Assessing Conceptual Level by the Paragraph Completion Method*. Toronto: Ontario Institute for Studies in Education, 1978.

Iazzetto, Demetria. *New Beginnings: A Handbook of Strategies for Women Returning to College*. Goddard College Graduate Program, May 1980.

Jensen, Glenn. "Education for Self-Fulfillment." In *Handbook of Adult Education*, edited by Robert M. Smith, George Aker, and Roby Kidd, pp. 513–26. New York: Macmillan, 1970.

Joyce, Bruce. "Learning How to Learn." *Theory Into Practice* 19(1981): 15–27.

Kagan, Jerome, et al. "Psychological Significance of Styles of Conceptualization." Edited by J. C. Wright and J. S. Kagan. *Basic Cognitive Processes in Children* 28(1963): 73–112. Monographs of the Society for Research in Child Development.

Kantor, Robert E. "The Affective Domain and Beyond." *Journal for the Study of Consciousness* 3(1974): 20–42.

Kazantzakis, Nikos. *Zorba the Greek*. New York: Simon and Schuster, 1952.

Kazworm, Carol E. "The Older Student as an Undergraduate." *Adult Education* 31(1980): 30–47.

Keen, Terry, and Pope, Maureen. *Personal Construct Theory in Education*. New York: Academic Press, 1981.

Kelly, George A. *The Psychology of Personal Constructs*. Vols. 1 and 2. New York: Norton, 1955.

Kidd, J. R. *How Adults Learn*. New York: Association Press, 1973.

Kirby, Patricia. *Cognitive Style, Learning Style, and Transfer Skill Acquisition*. Columbus, Ohio: National Center for Research in Vocational Education, 1979.

Knowles, Malcolm. *The Adult Learner: A Neglected Species*. Houston: Gulf Publishing Company, 1973.

————. *Self-Directed Learning*. New York: Association Press, 1975.

————. *A History of the Adult Education Movement in the United States*. Huntington, N.Y.: Robert E. Kreiger Company, 1977.

————. "How Do You Get People to Be Self-Directed Learners?" *Journal of Training and Development* 34(1980a): 96–99.

————. *The Modern Practice of Adult Education.* Rev. ed. Chicago: Follett Publishing Company, 1980b.

Knowles, Malcolm, and Knowles, Hulda. *Introduction to Group Dynamics.* Chicago: Follett Publishing Company, 1972.

Knox, Alan B. *Adult Development and Learning.* San Francisco: Jossey-Bass, 1977.

Knox, Alan B., ed. "Enhancing Proficiencies of Adult Educators." *New Directions for Continuing Education* 1(1979).

Kogan, Nathan. "Educational Implications of Cognitive Styles." In *Psychology and Educational Practice,* edited by Gerald S. Lesser. Glenview, Ill.: Scott Foresman, 1971.

Kolb, David A., and Fry, R. "Toward an Applied Theory of Experiential Learning." In *Theories of Group Process,* edited by C. L. Cooper. London: John Wiley, 1975.

Krishnamurti, Jiddu. *The Flight of the Eagle.* New York: Harper and Row, 1972.

Krumboltz, J. D. *Learning and the Educational Process.* Chicago: Rand McNally, 1965.

Kulich, Jindra. "An Historical Overview of the Adult Self-Learner." Paper read at the Northwest Institute on Independent Study, February 1970, at the University of British Columbia.

Laidlaw, Alexander F. *The Campus and the Community.* Montreal: Harvest House, 1961.

Lauffer, Armand. *Doing Continuing Education and Staff Development.* New York: McGraw-Hill, 1978.

Laurillard, Diana. "The Processes of Student Learning." *Higher Education* 8(1979): 395–409.

Lert, Erika Nagy. "Adult Second Language Acquisition: Laotian Hmong in Southland." Master's thesis, Brown University, 1980, ED 190728.

Lindeman, Eduard. *The Meaning of Adult Education.* New York: New Republic, Inc., 1926.

Little, David. "Adult Learning and Education: A Concept Analysis." Paper read at the Adult Education Research Conference, Adult Education Association of the U.S.A., April 1978, in San Antonio, Texas.

Loughary, John W., and Hopson, Barrie. *Producing Workshops, Seminars, and Short Courses: A Trainer's Handbook.* Chicago: Follett Publishing Company, 1979.

Loveall, Phillip. "The Relationship Between Cognitive Style and Achievement as Measured by the Old and New Forms of the GED." Unpublished doctoral dissertation, Northern Illinois University, 1979.

Luehrmann, Arthur. "Computer Illiteracy—A National Crisis and a Solution for it." *BYTE* 5(1980): 98–102.

Maloney, John D. "Developing Independent Learners in the Community College." In *Reading and the Adult Learner,* edited by Laura S. Johnson. Newark, Del.: International Reading Association, 1980, pp. 55–59.

Manzo, Anthony, et al. "Personality Characteristics and Learning Style Preferences of Adult Basic Education Students." Kansas City: University of Missouri College of Education, 1975.

Martens, Kay. "Cognitive Style: An Introduction with Annotated Bibliography." Paper read at the American College Personnel Association Convention, 1975, in Atlanta, Georgia.

Maslow, Abraham H. "Some Educational Implications of the Humanistic Psychologies." *Harvard Educational Review* 38(1968a): 685–96.

_____. *Toward a Psychology of Being.* New York: D. Van Nostrand, 1968b.

Mattis, Peter R. "The Learning to Learn Phenomenon as a Criterion for Testing the Effects of Desensitization with a 'Self' and an 'Other' Set." Unpublished doctoral dissertation, Ohio State University, 1968.

Maudsley, Donald B. "A Theory of Meta-Learning and Principles of Facilitation: An Organismic Perspective." Unpublished doctoral dissertation, University of Toronto, 1979.

Maxwell, Martha. *Improving Student Learning Skills.* San Francisco: Jossey-Bass, 1979.

McCarthy, Bernice. *The Four Mat System: Teaching to Learning Styles.* Arlington Heights, Ill.: Excel, 1980.

McClelland, David, et al. *The Achievement Motive.* New York: Appleton-Century-Crofts, 1953.

McCoy, Vivian Rogers, et al. *A Life Transition Reader.* Lawrence, Kans.: Adult life Resource Center, University of Kansas, 1980.

McCrosky, J. C., and Anderson, J. F. "The Relationship Between Communication Apprehension and Academic Achievement Among College Students." *Human Communication Research* 3(1976): 73–81.

McKenzie, Leon, ed. "Participation Training." *Viewpoints* Indiana University, School of Education 51(1975).

McKinley, John. *Participants Manual for Participation Training Institute.* Indianapolis: Consortium for Human Resources, 1978.
————. *Group Development Through Participation Training: A Trainer's Resource.* New York: Paulist Press, 1980.
McKinley, John, and Smith, Robert M. *Guide to Program Planning.* Greenwich, Conn: Seabury Press, 1965.
McLagan, Patricia A. *Helping Others Learn: Designing Programs for Adults.* Reading, Mass.: Addison-Wesley, 1978.
Merriam, Sharan B., and Cross, Laurence H. "Reminiscence and Life Satisfaction: The Potential for Educational Intervention." *Activities, Adaptation, and Aging,* in press.
Messick, Samuel, et al. *Individuality in Learning.* San Francisco: Jossey-Bass, 1976.
Mezirow, Jack. "Perspective Transformation." *Adult Education* 28(1978): 100–09.
Miller, Harry. *Teaching and Learning in Adult Education.* New York: Macmillan, 1964.
Moore, Michael G. "Learning Autonomy: The Second Dimension of Independent Learning." *Convergence* 5(1972): 76–87.
Mullally, Lee. "Educational Cognitive Style: Implications for Instructors." *Theory Into Practice* 16(1977): 238–42.

National Association of Secondary School Principals. *Student Learning Styles.* Reston, Va.: NASSP, 1979.
Niemi, John A., and Nagle, John M. "Learners, Agencies, and Program Development in Adult and Continuing Education." In *Managing Adult and Continuing Education Programs and Staff,* edited by P. D. Langerman and D. H. Smith, pp. 135–72. Washington, D.C.: National Association for Public Continuing and Adult Education, 1979.

Oen, Urban T. "Investigating the Interaction of Learning Styles and Types of Experiences in Vocational Technical Education." Appleton, Wis.: Fox Valley Technical Institute, 1973, ED 086 836.
Ommen, Jerome, et al. "Learning Preferences of Younger and Older Students." *Community College Frontiers* 8(1979): 29–33.
"On Mixing and Matching of Teaching and Learning Styles." *Practical Applications of Research* 3(1980): 1–4.
Ostrander, Sheila, and Schroeder, Lynn. *Superlearning.* New York: Dell, 1979.

Payton, Otto D., et al. "Learning Style Preference of Physical Therapy Students." *Physical Therapy* 59(1979): 147–52.

Peterson, Bernadine. "Adult Education by Means of Telephone." Paper read at the Adult Education Research Conference, February 1970, Minneapolis, Minn., ED 036 758.

Pfeiffer, J. William, and Jones, John E. *A Handbook of Structured Experiences for Human Relations Training.* San Diego, Calif.: University Associates, annually since 1972.

Pole, Thomas, *A History of the Origin and Progress of Adult Schools.* Bristol, England: C. McDowall, 1816.

Preising, Paul P., and Frost, Robert. "Increasing Student Retention Through Application of Attitude Change Packages (and) Increasing GPA and Student Retention of Low Income Minority Community College Students Through Application of Nightengale Conant Change Packages." Paper read at California Association for Institutional Research, May 1972, ED 076 188.

Quattrociocchi, Susan M. "Education, Employment and Income: The Financial Rewards of General Education and Vocational Education." *Lifelong Learning* 3(1980): 8–9.

Roberts, Thomas B. *Four Psychologies Applied to Education.* New York: John Wiley, 1975.

Robinson, Russell D. *Helping Adults Learn and Change.* Milwaukee: Omnibook Company, 1979.

Rogers, Carl. *Freedom to Learn.* Columbus, Ohio: Charles E. Merrill, 1969.

Rogers, Jennifer. *Adults Learning.* Baltimore, Md.: Penguin Books, 1971.

Rossman, Michael. "Learning Without a Teacher." Bloomington, Ind.: Phi Delta Kappa, 1973.

Säljo, Roger. "Learning About Learning." *Higher Education* 8(1979): 443–51.

Selz, N., and Ashley, W. L. "Teaching for Transfer: A Perspective." Columbus, Ohio: Ohio State University, The National Center for Research in Vocational Education, 1978.

Shah, Idries. *Learning How to Learn: Psychology and Spirituality in the Sufi Way.* London: Octagon Press, 1978.

Sheehy, Gail. *Passages: Predictable Crises of Adult Life.* New York: E. P. Dutton, 1976.

Sherriff, Dennis E. "A Factor Analysis Study of Hill's Cognitive Style Inventory." Unpublished doctoral dissertation, Texas A&M University, 1977.

Sherron, Ronald H., and Lumsden, D. Barry, eds. *Introduction to Educational Gerontology.* Washington, D.C.: Hemisphere, 1978.

Shuntich, M. E., and Kirkhorn, J. "Learning Styles Inventories and Self-Instructional Modules in Dental Auxiliary Education." Lexington, Ky.: University of Kentucky College of Allied Health Professions, August 1979.

Simons, George F. *Keeping Your Personal Journal.* New York: Paulist Press, 1978.

Skeen, Elois M. Evaluation Report of Niagara Falls. HEW 309 Project, 1975, ED 118 907.

Smith, Robert M. *Learning How to Learn in Adult Education.* DeKalb, Ill.: ERIC Clearinghouse in Career Education Information Series, no. 10: 1976, ED 132 245.

————. "Some Uses of Participation Training." *Adult Leadership* 18(1969): 77–78.

Smith, Robert M., and Haverkamp, Kay K. "Toward a Theory of Learning How to Learn." *Adult Education* 28(1977): 3–21.

Solomon, Daniel, et al. *Teaching Styles and Learning.* Chicago: Center for the Study of Liberal Education for Adults, 1963.

Stern, Milton R. "How to Use a Teacher." *Pleasures in Learning* New York University, School of Continuing Education 14(1966): 4–7.

Taylor, Marilyn. "Conceptual Representation of Learning from the Learner's Point of View." Proceedings of the Twenty-first Adult Education Research Conference, May 1980, Vancouver, B.C., pp. 193–98.

Thomas, Laurie F., and Harri-Augstein, Sheila. "The Self-Organized Learner and the Printed Word." Uxbridge, England: Brunel University, 1977, ED 159 594.

Thomas, Paul F. "The Influence of Dreams in the Personal Changes of Forty Adults." Unpublished doctoral dissertation, University of Toronto, 1978.

Toffler, Alvin. *Future Schock.* New York: Bantam, 1971.

Torbert, William. *Learning From Experience.* New York: Columbia University Press, 1972.

Tough, Allen M. *The Adult's Learning Projects.* 2nd edition. Austin, Tex.: Learning Concepts, 1979.

————. *Expand Your Life: A Pocket Book for Personal Change.* New York: College Entrance Examination Board, 1980.

————. *Intentional Changes: A Fresh Approach to Helping People Change.* Chicago: Follett Publishing Company, 1982.

Trecker, Harleigh B., and Trecker, Audrey R. *Working with Groups, Committees, and Communities.* Chicago: Follett Publishing Company, 1979.

Trillin, Alice Stewart, et al. *Teaching Basic Skills in College.* San Francisco: Jossey-Bass, 1980.

Ustinov, Peter. *Dear Me.* Boston: Little, Brown, 1977.

What I Have Learned: A Saturday Review Book. New York: Simon and Schuster, 1966.

"What is the Teacher Student Role in ABE?" Videotape. Owings Mills, Md.: Maryland State Department of Education, 1975.

Wilson, Robert R. "The Effects of Selected Programming—Analog Techniques and Voice Contact on Completion Behavior in Correspondence Education." Unpublished doctoral dissertation, University of Michigan, 1968.

Yanuzzi, Joan R. "An Experimental Study of the Effectiveness of a Course in Learning-to-Learn." Unpublished doctoral dissertation, Cornell University, 1967.

Zemke, Ron, and Nicholson, Delaine. "Suggestology: Will it Really Revolutionize Training?" *Training HRD,* January 1977, pp. 18–21.

Index

About the Author

Robert M. Smith, Professor of Adult Education at Northern Illinois University, has concentrated his teaching and writing for the past thirty years on the theories and practices of learning how to learn. From 1953 to 1967, he was part of the pioneering faculty group at Indiana University that developed Participation Training, the most effective and widely used system yet developed for imparting collaborative learning skills to adults. At NIU he has developed a popular forty-hour Learning How to Learn Lab that introduces the learning how to learn concept and teaches skills for self-directed learning, collaborative learning skills, and principles and methods for helping others develop such skills. Area residents as well as students participate. The Lab has become a mainstay of the graduate adult education program at the University.

Smith has been coeditor since 1978 of *Adult Education: A Journal of Research and Theory.* He also is the coauthor of *Adult Education Procedures* (Seabury 1963), senior editor of *The Handbook of Adult Education* (Macmillan 1970), and author of *Learning How to Learn in Adult Education* (ERIC Clearinghouse, 1976). His articles have appeared in a wide variety of professional journals.

In addition to his university work, Smith has served as consultant and evaluator for adult education and training programs for industry, labor unions, schools and colleges, churches, hospitals, libraries, voluntary agencies, and entrepreneurial schools. He also served as an adult education advisor in three African countries for the State Department. He earned his Ph.D. in comparative literature from Indiana University and has been awarded Distinguished Service citations from both the Indiana Association for Adult Education and the Adult Education Association of the U.S.A.